Teaching Phonics, Phonemic Awareness, and Word Recognition

Ashley Bishop, Ed.D
Suzanne Bishop, M.E.D.

Teacher Created Materials, Inc.

Cover design by Darlene Spivak

www.teachercreated.com

Made in U.S.A.

ISBN 1-57690-126-2

Order Number TCM 2126

Table of Contents

Introduction

My wife asked me to write the introduction to this book. She did so for a very special reason. What we have written in this book has great significance to me. My elementary school years were not the most pleasant of experiences. I took the first grade once, was asked to participate in the second grade twice, and based on my academic performance, it would not have been inappropriate to have taken the third grade three times. By the time I arrived at the sixth grade, I was a charter member of the low group and developed the attitude that reading was an activity to avoid at all cost. In fact, I viewed reading only as a series of skills that resulted in failure. Obviously, reading was my least favorite subject. Fortunately, it was in the sixth grade that Mr. Winters made the decision that I could and would read.

One day while I was leaping benches during the lunch hour (unfortunately, students were still sitting at the benches), my sixth grade teacher, Mr. Winters, noticed my interest in hurdling. That very day, he presented me with a book about a track star with perfect hurdling form who wanted to win the city championships. That afternoon, at the end of the school day, he read the first chapter to me and then sent both me and the book home. Let me say I wanted to read that book! I struggled through it three times until I could understand every wonderful concept and every bit of action presented. I was hooked, and Mr. Winters had more bait. He presented me with one sport book after another and then introduced me to the library. He told me I could read any book in this place of knowledge if I would just take the time to really learn the skills of reading. I could read anything, find out anything, and I could do it myself!

My remembrances lead me to the point of *Teaching Phonics, Phonemic Awareness, and Word Recognition.* Students see little reason to learn about schwas, digraphs, and diphthongs. They want to read books about large red dogs, curious monkeys, and teachers who come from black lagoons. Great literature motivates children to learn important and necessary decoding skills. If students are going to develop the richest possible "logic of the code," we must give them both reasons and skills to do so.

Ashley Bishop

Overview of Phonics, Phonemic Awareness, and Word Recognition

History

We wrote this book for a very pragmatic reason. We want students, when encountering unfamiliar words, to have all the skills necessary to pronounce and understand them. We do not care if they learn the skills implicitly or explicitly or in a whole-language or skill-based classroom. Students need to develop their own logic of how the code process works and have the desire and confidence to use the process whenever it is needed. We do have a bias about the environment in which to best teach students the necessary decoding skills. It is a balanced environment where students are given authentic reasons to read and write and are systematically provided with instruction that allows them to do so. We are tired of the "great debate" about whether or not to teach phonics, and have been for some time. In a Reading Teacher article entitled "My Daughter Learns to Read" (Bishop, 1978), we asked educators to "neither simpleminded nor muddleheaded be." Our concern was this—"As

> **Students need to develop their own logic of how the code process works and have the desire and confidence to use the process whenever it is needed.**

1

we put added emphasis on the basics, there are teachers forgetting to give students a reason for reading. This is being simpleminded. Supplying students with a set of skills does not necessarily produce readers. On the flip side of the coin, there are teachers who feel that all you must do is put a book in students' hands, love them, read to them often, and they will learn to read. These teachers have forgotten the necessity of using skills in reading. This is being muddleheaded" (Bishop, 1978, p. 6).

Simpleminded and muddleheaded are strong terms to use, but they reflect the degree of our disenchantment in 1978 and our disenchantment today over the bitterness of the decoding debate. Can we forget the debate and, instead, remember the children?

Supplying students with a set of skills does not necessarily produce readers.

The title of this text, *Teaching Phonics, Phonemic Awareness, and Word Recognition* accurately reflects its content. To be successful readers, students must develop their own understanding of how our language works and then be able to decode so fluently and naturally that all attention is given to understanding what is being read. This happens best when students have been systematically taught all the skills necessary for successful decoding. This book presents these skills.

We will begin with a general overview of the reading and writing process and follow with two precursors to the decoding process—phonemic awareness and knowledge of the alphabet. We will then discuss phonics, structural analysis, sight words, and context. Each chapter, beginning with Phonemic Awareness, will have basically the same organizational format. An overview of the topic will be presented, followed by instructional activities and a list of appropriate children's literature to use during instruction.

The Reading and Writing Process

Printed Language

To appropriately discuss the roles phonics, phonemic awareness, and word recognition play in the reading process, it is important to have a clear understanding of what authors do as they engage in the writing process and what readers do as they engage in the reading process.

Authors have thoughts, ideas, feelings, and concerns. They turn all these concepts into language and put this language down on the printed page. Readers have to lift this printed language up off the page and interact with the ideas being presented, as well as construct new and personalized meaning. We say, then, that reading is a process of active communication where readers construct knowledge from an author's printed language.

Reading is an act of constructing knowledge from what is read. There is a variety of processes in which readers must engage to be successful.

Readers have to lift this printed language up off the page and interact with the ideas being presented, as well as construct new and personalized meaning.

3

◆ Reading as a language process

Readers are communicating with an author's printed language. To be able to read, one must have language. The more this language is like that of the author, the greater the chance that active communication will take place.

◆ Reading as a thinking process

Without thinking, active communication cannot take place. Active communication is the process where readers seek meaning. When the meaning being sought is personally valuable, the reading process is more active. In short, readers have questions they want answered. In fact, one of the significant differences between good readers and poor readers is that good readers have a personal stake in their reading. They are involved in the process because they want to be. They read because they want to be entertained or have questions they want answered. If there is one statement that summarizes good readers, it is this—Good readers ask questions. Of course, the questions they should ask are questions that move their thinking well beyond the literal level. The ultimate questions they can ask are often, "What is the author's purpose in writing this?" and "How effectively did the author achieve this purpose?" This is sophisticated thinking, but young readers do it all the time. When they say, "I like Clifford books. They are funny," students are understanding that the author's purpose was to entertain. When they say, "I want to read more books by Norman Bridwell," they are stating that they think he is an effective writer.

◆ Reading as a decoding process

Readers must have a variety of tools to lift the author's printed language up off the page. Decoding supplies students with such tools. When students use context clues, phonics, and structural analysis, as well as a rich store of sight words to the page, they have the resources to change printed language into thoughts and ideas with which they can communicate. Ultimately, the decoding process should be so natural and fluent that all attention can be given to understanding what is read.

◆ Reading as a personal process

Reading is one of the more personal processes in which individuals can engage. The meaning readers take away from the printed page is often unique. The more the reader's knowledge of the world is like that of the author, the more easily communication will take place. Also, reading is a personal process in relation to the physical and mental health of readers. When students are feeling good, both mentally and physically, reading is a less difficult task. When they

> **Active communication is the process where readers seek meaning.**

are tired, hungry, and unsure of themselves, communicating with printed language can appear to be an overwhelming task. We have all found studying for the third final in a row to be a significant challenge in the best of cases, and almost impossible when we lacked sleep, proper nutrition, and confidence. Finally, students' attitudes toward reading and their views of themselves as readers make reading very much a personal process. When students walk into our classrooms and say, "Wow, a new book by Jack Prelutsky! Can I read it?" we know we have students who view themselves as readers.

◆ Reading as a constructive process

One of the most important results of the reading process is that readers leave the printed page with more knowledge than they bring to it. For this to happen, students must bring experiences, concepts, language, and motivation to the reading task and use each of these to test what they are reading against what they already know and would like to learn. As students say, "This makes sense," "I didn't know this," or "This is just what I needed to know," they are constructing knowledge. This is the heart of the reading process.

The Components of Reading

Reading, for discussion purposes, can be broken into two major components: decoding and comprehension. Decoding and comprehension seem to be mutually enriching tasks, and, while it is often difficult to separate the two, they will be discussed separately.

Decoding

The skills of decoding can be placed into broad categories: phonics, structural analysis, sight words, and context clues.

Phonics is the association of sounds with symbols. The printed word *cat* is made up of three symbols, the letters of the alphabet "c," "a," and "t." Students using phonics attach the sounds /k/, /a/, and /t/ to these symbols. Because our alphabet consists of consonants and vowels, phonics is the process of giving sounds to single consonants, consonant clusters, single vowels, and vowel clusters.

Structural analysis is the analysis of the structure of a word. While phonics is reasonably successful with single syllable words, it begins to break down with multi-syllabic words. Consequently, the task of structural analysis is to break large words into more manageable units. For example, when seeing the word *cowboy* for the first time, students will often notice the smaller units *cow* and *boy*. The term "morphemic analysis" is often used in place of structural analysis.

One of the most important results of the reading process is that readers leave the printed page with more knowledge than they brought to it.

5

The definition of sight words rivals the logic of the definition of structural analysis. Sight words are words that are recognized immediately without need of analysis. Sight words are important for a variety of reasons, but the most significant reason is that a strong majority of the words students frequently encounter cannot be sounded out. Words such as *was*, *said*, *the*, and *to* do not effectively subject themselves to the use of phonics.

Context clues is the use of the print surrounding an unfamiliar word to give it meaning and to help pronounce it. When students are reading a sentence, "The _____ is a lizard that changes color," they quite often will put in *chameleon* because they know the word makes sense.

Ultimately, we want to produce readers who use decoding skills so naturally and fluently that all their attention can be given to gathering meaning from what they are reading. For this to happen, students need to understand the process so well they develop their own logic of the code. No two students approach an unknown word exactly alike. They take the tools they have been taught and use the ones that make most sense and work best for them to personalize the process. It is our task to ensure that students have been taught all essential decoding options so that the personal logic of the code process they develop is as rich as possible.

Comprehension

Comprehension is the heart of the reading process. When involved in the comprehension process, students are testing what they are reading against what they already know. Stated another way, comprehension results from the interaction between the information in the text and the prior knowledge readers bring to the text. This is the act of comprehension or the process of constructing knowledge. As students comprehend, they need to do so at three levels, each more important than the one preceding it.

Reading the Lines

Reading the lines is the process of comprehending at the "who," "what," "where," and "when" level. It is the understanding of explicitly stated information. The often asked question, "Who is buried in Grant's tomb?" or "What color is Clifford, the dog?" are reading the lines level questions. These types of questions are lower-level questions and often labeled literal reading. Students can function at this level quite successfully and still not really understand what they are reading.

Reading Between the Lines

Reading between the lines is often labeled interpretive reading, and it is at this level that critical or higher-order thinking takes place. Students functioning at this level make inferences about implicit text information. Answering the question, "Which of the three little pigs is the smartest?" when the answer is not explicitly stated in the story, is an example of reading between the lines.

Reading Beyond the Lines

Reading beyond the lines asks students to step outside the story and view it from another perspective. There is a variety of components of reading beyond the lines. They are often labeled application, creative, critical, and evaluative reading.

♦ Application reading is the process of using what is gained from the text material in a real-life situation or comparing what is learned to other text material.

♦ Creative reading is the process of manipulating the story in creative ways. Coming up with another ending to a story, seeing the story from a different perspective, or changing the personality of the main character and seeing how this might change the direction of the story are all creative endeavors.

♦ Critical reading, in its richest form, is understanding the author's purpose. "Why is the author writing this?" is an important critical level question for readers to ask.

♦ Evaluative reading is making a judgment on how effectively the author did what he or she wanted to do.

An important concept to remember is that comprehension is what reading is about.

Combining these last two levels of comprehension, it can be said that a critical-evaluative reader is one who understands what the author was doing and how effectively the author did it. This is truly higher-order thinking.

Concluding Remarks

In review, the components of reading are comprehension and decoding. They are often difficult to separate and are mutually enriching tasks. An important concept to remember is that comprehension is what reading is about. Students must read for meaning. That is, they must acknowledge and anticipate that they are reading to gain information.

Decoding is a tool that is learned and used to help one comprehend. It is a necessary skill that assists readers in identifying unknown words. It must be accompanied by a quest for comprehension if reading is to be a meaningful experience. Too often, students become engrossed with the task of decoding and lose sight of the purpose—to look for meaning. As teachers, we must ensure that students develop an appreciation for reading and recognize that while decoding is important, it is only one part of the process. Both skills, decoding and comprehension, are vital for success.

Phonemic Awareness

The Next Step

We must remember that one goal of phonics instruction is to assist students in understanding the relationship between printed letters and speech sounds. Thus, in this chapter, we will discuss the concept of phonemic awareness—awareness of the sounds in our language. It will be followed by a chapter that focuses on printed letters—our alphabet. These two chapters must precede a discussion on phonics if we want to develop a rich understanding of the process students go through as they associate sounds (phonemes) with symbols (graphemes).

To begin a chapter on phonemic awareness we need to define it and stress its importance. The definition is fairly straightforward. Phonemic awareness is the awareness that sounds are in our language and that spoken words are made up of individual sounds. Adams (1990) tells us that it is not a working knowledge of phonemes that is so important, but conscious, analytic knowledge. It is neither the ability to hear the differences between two phonemes nor the ability to distinctly produce them that is significant. What is important is the awareness that they exist as abstract and manipulative components of our language. Developmentally, this awareness

Phonemic awareness is the awareness that sounds are in our language and that spoken words are made up of individual sounds.

9

seems to depend upon the child's inclination or encouragement to lend conscious attention to the sounds, as distinct from the meaning, of words.

The importance of phonemic awareness to reading success cannot be stressed too strongly. Research has shown repeatedly that phonics is a potent predictor of success in learning to read (Adams, 1990; Stanovich, 1986; Yopp, 1988; Yopp, 1995b). Stanovich (1986) tells us that phonemic awareness is more highly related to reading success than students' scores on intelligence and reading readiness tests and on their listening/comprehension performance. What is exciting about phonemic awareness, given its importance, is that it can be developed in students through training. Yopp (1992) suggests the following progression in phonemic awareness training.

The importance of phonemic awareness to reading success cannot be stressed too strongly.

Guide students to...

1. hear rhymes or alliteration.
2. blend sounds to make a spoken word.
3. count phonemes in spoken words.
4. identify the beginning, middle, and final sounds in spoken words.
5. substitute one phoneme for another.
6. delete phonemes from words.
7. segment words into phonemes.

This is labeled a progression because each task is somewhat more challenging than the task preceding it. Students should be taken through this progress in preschool, kindergarten, and early first grade. However, a small number of students may need phonemic training well into their school years. A word of caution. While we are suggesting that some students be trained in phonemic knowledge, we are not suggesting word/sound drills and worksheets. What we are suggesting is language play, fully immersing children in rhymes, rhythms, word play, and rich predictable literature. The following section will present activities that develop phonemic awareness in children.

This is an appropriate point at which to state our appreciation for the work Hallie Yopp, a colleague at California State University, Fullerton, has done in the area of phonemic awareness. She is one of the leading authorities in this important field in the United States. We have borrowed heavily from her work on phonemic awareness and are thankful for the depth of her efforts.

Strategies for Developing Phonemic Awareness

The two activities presented relate to steps two and four of the seven step progression presented earlier. The first activity is a blending activity. Yopp (1992) tells us that blending requires students to manipulate individual sounds by combining them to form a word. We suggest teachers develop a deck of picture cards featuring familiar animals. The cards are placed face down, and the teacher selects one at a time. Without letting students see the cards, the teacher pronounces the isolated sounds that name the pictures, for example, /d/-/o/-/g/. After the children blend the sounds and guess the word, the picture is shown to affirm their response. This also makes a nice warm-up to subjects and characters in a new story the students are going to hear.

The second strategy is a sound isolation activity where students are asked to identify the sounds in a spoken word. In this activity, students are sung a song that encourages them to think about sounds in words. The teacher may choose to emphasize a single sound throughout the song, or each verse may focus on a different sound. Songs can also focus on medial or final sounds. The following verse, sung to the tune of "Old MacDonald Had a Farm," is an excellent example of the process.

The teacher may choose to emphasize a single sound through-out the song, or each verse may focus on a different sound.

> What's the sound that starts these words:
> *Turtle*, *time*, and *teeth*?
> /t/ is the sound that starts these words:
> *Turtle*, *time*, and *teeth*.
> With a /t/, /t/ here, and a /t/, /t/ there,
> Here a /t/, there a /t/, everywhere a /t/, /t/.
> /t/ is the sound that starts these words:
> *Turtle*, *time*, and *teeth*!

(Yopp, 1992, p. 700)

Assessing Phonemic Awareness

Yopp developed the Yopp-Singer test of phonemic awareness. Yopp indicates that students who segment all or nearly all of the items correctly are probably phonemically aware. While the test is presented on the following page, we strongly suggest that teachers looking to use the test read the complete article, "A Test for Assessing Phonemic Awareness in Young Children" (Yopp, 1995b).

Yopp-Singer Test of Phoneme Segmentation

Student's name _____ Date _____

Score (number correct) _____

Directions: Today we're going to play a word game. I'm going to say a word and I want you to break the word apart. You are going to tell me each sound in the word in order. For example, if I say "old," you should say "/o/-/l/-/d/." *(Administrator: Be sure to say the sounds, not the letters, in the word.)* Let's try a few together.

Practice items: *ride, go, man (Assist the child in segmenting these items as necessary.)*

Test items: *(Circle those items that the student correctly segments; incorrect responses may be recorded on the blank line following the item.)*

1. dog _____	12. lay _____
2. keep _____	13. race _____
3. fine _____	14. zoo _____
4. no _____	15. three _____
5. she _____	16. job _____
6. wave _____	17. in _____
7. grew _____	18. ice _____
8. that _____	19. at _____
9. red _____	20. top _____
10. me _____	21. by _____
11. sat _____	22. do _____

The author, Hallie Kay Yopp, California State University, Fullerton, grants permission for this test to be reproduced. The author acknowledges the contribution of the late Harry Singer to the development of this test.

Literature Which Promotes Phonemic Awareness

As will be the strategy throughout this book, we will provide a list of children's books which enhance the skill being discussed. The following are some of our favorites for promoting phonemic awareness. For a comprehensive selection, we suggest the article, "Read-Aloud Books for Developing Phonemic Awareness: An Annotated Bibliography," by Hallie Yopp (1995a).

Buller, J. & Schade, S. (1988, Simon & Schuster). *I Love You, Good Night*. A mother and child tell each other how much they love one another with phrases such as, "as much as pigs love pies" and "as much as frogs love flies."

Deming, A. G. (1994, Puffin). *Who Is Tapping at My Window?* A young girl hears a tapping at her window and asks, "Who is there?" The animals respond. The loon is followed by the raccoon; the dog is followed by the frog.

Geraghty, P. (1992, Crown Books). *Stop That Noise!* A mouse is annoyed with a noisy forest. The presentation of animal and machine noise draw attention to the sounds of our language.

Gordon, J. (1993, Puffin). *Six Sleepy Sheep*. Six sheep try to fall asleep by slurping celery soup and sipping simmered milk. Students become aware of the /s/ sound.

Krauss, R. (1992, Western Publishing). *I Can Fly*. In this simple book, a child imitates the actions of a variety of animals. "A cow can moo. I can too." On the final page, nonsense words that rhyme are used, encouraging listeners to experiment with sounds. "Gubble gubble gubble, I'm a mubble in a pubble."

Lewison, W. (1992, Scholastic). *Buzz Said the Bee*. A series of animals sit on top of each other. Before each animal climbs on top, it does something that rhymes with the animal it approaches. The hen dances a jig on the pig.

Otto, C. (1993, HarperCollins). *Dinosaur Chase*. A mother dinosaur reads her child a story about dinosaurs. Both alliteration and rhyme are used.

Silverstein, S. (1964, HarperCollins). *A Giraffe and a Half*. Using cumulative and rhyming patterns, this story is about a giraffe who has a rose on his nose, a bee on his knee, etc.

As will be the strategy throughout this book, we will provide a list of children's books which enhance the skill under discussion.

Slepian, J. & Seidler, A. (1988, Scholastic). *The Hungry Thing*. A hungry thing wants to be fed things like shmancakes and tickles. The townspeople have to figure out what it is he wants to eat.

We would be remiss if we did not include some of our favorite books of poetry in this section. Reading students rich and wonderful poetry is an excellent and natural way to develop phonemic awareness. The following is a list of our favorites.

Bennett, J.	*Tiny Tim* (1982, Delacorte)
dePaola, T.	*Tomie dePaola's Mother Goose* (1985, Putnam)
de Regniers, B., Schenk, B. White, M. & Bennett, J.	*Sing a Song of Popcorn* (1988, Scholastic)
Hopkins, L. B.	*Surprises* (1986, HarperCollins)
Hopkins, L. B.	*The Sky is Full of Song* (1987, HarperCollins)
Larrick, N.	*When the Dark Comes Dancing* (1983, Putnam)
Oxenbury, H.	*The Helen Oxenbury Nursery Story Book* (1985, Knopf)
Prelutsky, J.	*The Random House Book of Poetry for Children* (1983, Random House)
Prelutsky, J.	*Read Aloud Rhymes for the Very Young* (1986, Knopf)
Prelutsky, J.	*Something Big Has Been Here* (1990, Greenwillow)
Silverstein, S.	*Where the Sidewalk Ends* (1986, Dell)

Reading students rich and wonderful poetry is an excellent and natural way to develop phonemic awareness.

Poetry is especially effective when it is introduced in harmony with the season. The following page has an excellent example for November harvest poetry.

Harvest Poetry

The Food Guide Pyramid

If you want to be healthy and strong,
Just eat this way, you cannot go wrong.
From breads, cereal, pasta, and rice,
Six to eleven servings are nice.
And from all the fruits there are to eat,
Two to four servings are quite a treat.
Three to five form the vegetable group
Would make a lovely vegetable soup.
From poultry, fish, beans, eggs, nuts, and meat,
Two to three servings are fine to eat.
Milk, yogurt, and cheese are good for you;
Two to three servings would nicely do.
Fats, oils, and sweets, please use sparingly;
Other foods have them naturally.
Just follow this list all the way through—
To make a healthier, happier you!

Delicious and Nutritious

Can you believe it's really true
That all these foods are good for you?
Speckled strawberries, plump and sweet,
Juicy oranges, a tasty treat,
A hot fresh slice of homemade bread,
Apples of the rosiest red,
A tall, cool glass of creamy milk,
Some mashed potatoes, smooth as silk,
Tangy yogurt with fruit on top,
Two scrambled eggs, so piping hot,
A heaping plate of spaghetti,
Corn on the cob—are you ready?
Raisins, melons, grapes, plums, and cheese,
Chicken fricassee, if you please,
Fruit and cereal in a bowl,
Graham crackers until I'm full,
Brown rice and banana nut bread,
Frozen juice bars, purple and red,
Peanuts, walnuts, coconut, too,
Oh, I can't wait! How about you?

The Scarecrow and the Raven

Said the scarecrow to the raven,
"Is it corn that you are cravin?"
"No, no, not I," replied the crow.
"Hay is the only way I go."
"But hay's the thing inside of me!
Surely there's something else you see!"
"No, you'll make a tasty dinner,
And, just think, you'll be much thinner!"

Reprinted from TCM 862 November Monthly Activities—Early Childhood, *Teacher Created Materials, 1996*

Concluding Remarks

We cannot stress too heavily the importance of phonemic awareness to students' reading success. Stanovich (1986) has implied that phonemic awareness is the most important pedagogical breakthrough of this century. However, learning the sounds of our language is not enough to enhance reading success. Students must also have symbols to attach to these sounds. This will be discussed at length in the next chapter.

The Alphabet

Overview

As students gain an awareness of the sounds of our language, they need to become comfortable with the letters of the alphabet. Students need to recognize upper and lower case letters and recognize the letters in a rich variety of settings. Students will ultimately be attaching sounds to the letters of the alphabet as they engage in the process called phonics. As phonics is a sound/symbol activity, students' chances of success in this endeavor are greatly increased when both the sounds and symbols (alphabet) are familiar friends. In introducing the teaching of the alphabet, let us first present an assessment process for alphabet knowledge. Strategies for teaching the letters of the alphabet will follow. The chapter will conclude with an excellent list of children's alphabet books to read to students.

As students gain an awareness of the sounds of our language, they need to become comfortable with the letters of the alphabet.

Assessing Knowledge of the Alphabet

We have developed a quick and easy assessment process to examine students' knowledge of the alphabet. The letters of the alphabet are placed in random order in two groups. The first group has the alphabet in lowercase letters and the second group has the alphabet in uppercase letters. The following is an example:

e	t	a	l	d	v	o	m	p
b	n	f	j	h	g	w	k	s
x	i	u	r	z	q	c	y	

B	N	F	J	H	G	W	K	S
X	I	U	R	Z	Q	C	Y	P
E	T	A	L	D	V	O	M	

Once assessment of students' needs has been accomplished, the instructional task becomes more efficient and effective.

The teacher should make one master copy for all students to examine and one copy (per student) to record student responses on. The test should be given to students individually. There are two components to the process.

Ask a student to look at the master copy and say the name of each lower and uppercase letter. On the student's individual copy, mark a plus if he or she gives the correct response. Mark an incorrect response to the right of the stimulus letter. If the student names all letters correctly, stop the assessment process because the student knows the letters of the alphabet. If the student has difficulty, try saying the letters of the alphabet out loud in random order. Do this with both lower and uppercase letters. Mark a plus to the right of all letters the student points to correctly. If the student cannot locate the letter, put a check to the right.

If the student is successful with this approach, he or she has a working knowledge of the alphabet but needs ongoing reinforcement and practice with the letters. If the student has difficulty with both components, the target letters for further instruction are identified.

Once assessment of student needs has been accomplished, the instructional task becomes more efficient and effective.

Strategies for Developing Knowledge of the Alphabet

Adams (1990) supplies us with an important consideration when decisions are made as to how to teach the alphabet. She makes this statement, "The ability to name and recognize letters is, in general, not established through showing the children the letters and then teaching them the names. That's backwards. Most children are taught the letters only after they know their names. By thoroughly learning the names first, the child has a solid mnemonic peg to which the precept of the letter can be connected as it is built. By thoroughly teaching the names first, the teacher can methodically exploit them toward developing the child's sense of the functionally equivalent and distinctive differences between characters" (p. 359).

Toward this end, we have supplied a variety of alphabet books that should be read to students on a regular basis so that they are familiar with the names of the alphabet letters. It is the rare student who does not enjoy Bill Martin, Jr. and John Archambault's *Chicka Chicka Boom Boom* (Simon & Schuster, 1989). The pure joy of saying "A told B and B told C, I'll meet you at the top of the coconut tree," helps make the alphabet a well-known acquaintance rather than something to be feared. It is also important not to forget an old friend, "The Alphabet Song." This is something all students enjoy. Singing it on a consistent basis certainly gets students comfortable with the names of the letters.

Students should begin writing words with the letters they have learned as early as possible.

Once students know the alphabet letter names, the next step is an obvious one. They need to learn to recognize each letter and attach the name they have already learned. To do this, we must decide on the appropriate order in which to teach the letters. Manzo and Manzo (1995) report there are four groups of letters that tend to produce confusion for students and therefore should not be taught at the same time.

1. e, a, s, c, o
2. b, d, p, o, g, h
3. f, l, t, k, i, h
4. n, m, u, h, r

While this is important information to know, personal experience has found that teaching the letters of the alphabet students find personally valuable first is the most successful approach. Students learn best, and often easiest, the letters of their own names. And, when a class has Bill, Betty, Belinda, and Bobby as members, it would seem remiss not to introduce the letter "B" and its name early in the instructional process. Students should begin writing words with the letters they have learned as early as possible. However, having students copy or trace long lists of letters is not the answer. In relationship to this statement, we find Adams (1990) supplies some important information. "Copying, of course, must be used; it is a necessary step toward the independent printing of a letter. But it appears that neither tracing nor copying, but independent printing holds the greatest leverage for perceptual and motor learning of letter shapes" (p. 364). Teach students that they have important things to write and that knowing the alphabet allows them to write these important things. Encourage invented spelling if necessary. Invented spelling is an excellent indicator that students are phonemically aware and are often ready to formally begin learning phonics.

Alphabet Books

Earlier, we mentioned reading alphabet books to students. The following is a list of our favorite choices. For a more comprehensive selection, we suggest examining Chaney's (1993) "Alphabet Books: Resources for Learning."

> **Invented spelling is an excellent indicator that students are phonemically aware and are often ready to formally begin learning phonics.**

Mitsumaso, A.	*Anno's Alphabet: An Adventure in Imagination* (1975, HarperCollins)
Base, G.	*Animalia* (1987, Abrams)
Bayer, J.	*A, My Name is Alice* (1984, Dial Books)
Bragg, R. G.	*Alphabet Out Loud* (1991, Picture Book Studio)
Ehlert, L.	*Eating the Alphabet: Fruits and Vegetables from A to Z* (1989, Harcourt, Brace, & Jovanovich)
Hoban, T.	*26 Letters and 99 Cents* (1987, Greenwillow)
Kitchen, B.	*Animal Alphabet* (1984, Dial)
Martin, B., Jr. & Archambault, J.	*Chicka Chicka Boom Boom* (1989, Simon & Schuster)
Van Allsburg, C.	*The Z was Zapped* (1987, Houghton Mifflin)
Wormell, C.	*An Alphabet of Animals* (1990, Dial)
Yolen, J.	*All in the Woodland Early: An ABC Book* (1991, Boyd Mills)

Concluding Remarks

At this point, students should have a firm knowledge of the alphabet. Also, they should be aware of the sounds of our language. Then, it is time for them to become aware of the alphabetic principle—to realize that the alphabet letters not only have names, but they also have sounds. Once students realize this, they need a variety of opportunities to write the language. It is time to start explicitly teaching them the phonic skills necessary for effective reading.

Phonics

Introduction

We are going to begin by making an unusual statement. Phonics does not work very well. Now that we have your attention, it seems important to state that while phonics does not work very well, it is still a useful and important tool in a young reader's cadre of decoding options. How can we say that phonics does not work well, and yet it is an important decoding tool? Let us begin by discussing why it does not always work well.

"In some languages, such as Finnish, there is a neat one-to-one correspondence between sound and spelling. A /k/ to the Finns is always "k," and /l/ eternally and comfortingly "l." But in English, pronunciation is so various—one might say random—that not one of the twenty-six letters can be relied on for constancy. Either they clasp to themselves a variety of pronunciations, as with the "c" in *race*, *rack*, and *rich*, or they sulk in silence, like the "b" in *debt*, the "a" in *bread*, and the second "t" in *thistle*. In combinations they become even more unruly and unpredictable, most famously in the letter cluster "ough," which can be pronounced in any of eight ways—as in *through, though, thought, tough, plough, thorough, hiccough,* and *lough* (an English word for lake or loch, pronounced

How can we say that phonics does not work well, and yet it is an important decoding tool?

roughly as the latter). The pronunciation possibilities are so various that probably not one English speaker in a hundred could pronounce with confidence the name of a crowlike bird called a *chough*. (It's chuff.) Two words in English, *hegemony* and *phthisis*, have nine pronunciations each. But perhaps nothing speaks more clearly for the absurdities of English pronunciation than the word for the study of pronunciation in English, *orthoepy*, can itself be pronounced two ways" (Bryson, 1990, p. 85).

In *Beginning to Read: Thinking and Learning About Print*, Adams states, "As material to be taught or learned, individual letter-sound correspondence and phonic generalizations are inherently intractable when divorced from the rest of the reading situation. They are abstract, piecemeal, unorderable, unreliable, barely numerable, and sometimes mutually incompatible" (Adams, 1990, p. 291). Why would Adams, a supporter of having students explicitly taught phonics, make such a statement?

Let us examine the word *phonics* from a sound-symbol perspective and the word from left to right, as many young readers would.

Let us examine the word *phonics* from a sound-symbol perspective and the word from left to right, as many young readers would. We will do this in a question and answer format.

What sound does the first letter of *phonics* make?

Unfortunately, the "p" does not make a sound in the word *phonics*.

What sound does the "h" make?

It, like the "p," does not make a sound in the word *phonics*.

Can the "p" and "h" be put together?

Yes, but when put together, neither the sound of "p" nor the sound of "h" is heard. Instead, the /f/ sound is heard.

What sound does the vowel "o" make? Does it make the long vowel sound, as heard in *oak*, or the short vowel sound, as heard in *hot*? It makes the short vowel sound as heard in *hot*. However, it is not an easy sound to distinguish in the middle of a word such as *phonics*.

What sound does the letter "c" make? Does it ever have its own sound like we think of most consonants having?

It does not have its own sound. Instead, it produces either the /k/ or the /s/ sound. In the word *phonics*, the "c" produces the /k/ sound.

As can be seen, the sound-symbol process is not a perfect one, not even with an important word like *phonics*, the label used for the process. Now, try to associate sounds with the symbols (letters) of much more interesting words. To most adults, and certainly to students, names are very important. And, as names come from a variety of different cultures using different languages, the sounds traditionally associated with symbols often just do not work. Stop reading this text for a moment and give phonics a try with your own name or, if you teach, the names on your class roster.

If you did pause to give phonics a try with your name, you are probably in agreement with our initial statement that phonics does not always work well. If this is the case, how can it also be stated that phonics is an important decoding tool? We will spend the rest of this chapter supplying an answer.

Two important statements need to be made about phonics.

1. Phonics is a necessary component of the reading process.
2. Phonics instruction, by itself, is not sufficient to produce effective readers.

While phonics does not work as well as we would like, it works well enough to assist students as they seek meaning. However, phonics is just one component of the reading process. Producing students who can use the sound-symbol process, while important, is not sufficient for producing good readers. This chapter has been organized so all aspects of phonics are presented. It starts with a short history.

Phonics: A Short History

Phonics skills—should we, or should we not, teach them? And if we should teach them, how should they be taught? These are not new questions. In fact, they have been asked since children were first taught to read. It is not inappropriate to state that the debate over teaching phonics has been long and often acrimonious. Beginning in the Middle Ages, when the first primers were introduced, the teaching of reading generally followed a part-to-whole process. The alphabet was taught first, followed by sounds (often using target words), and then syllables and short words. This practice continued well into the 1800s. However, in 1840 the pendulum began to shift toward the whole-word method, and the debate became heated.

According to Nila Banton Smith, *My Little Primer*, written in 1840 by Josiah Bumstead, was the first reader to be based specifically on

As can be seen, the sound-symbol process is not a perfect one, not even with an important word like "phonics," the label used for the process.

the look-say method. Bumstead expressed the justification for his method as follows:

> In teaching reading, the general practice has been to begin with the alphabet, and drill the child upon the letters, month after month, until he is supposed to have acquired them. This method, so irksome and vexatious to both teacher and scholar, is now giving place to another, which experience has proven to be more philosophical, intelligent, pleasant, and rapid. It is that of beginning with familiar and easy words, instead of letters (Smith, 1967, p. 87).

A close reading of *Why Johnny Can't Read* reveals an often simplistic view of the reading process.

Bumstead presented his case gently in comparison to Horace Mann (Balmuth, 1982). Horace Mann, an early advocate of public school education, became disenchanted with phonics and stressed that children be taught rich, meaningful words rather than letters, those "skeleton-shaped, bloodless, ghostly apparitions" (Balmuth, 1982, p. 190). Gradually, the influence of a whole-word approach grew and received its most encouraging support in 1908 when Huey, in *The Psychology and Pedagogy of Reading,* reported on research he had conducted. Huey found that when adults looked at individual letters, and then four, eight, and twelve letter words, the multiplication of letters made proportionately little difference in the ease or speed of recognition. Based on this evidence, he argued that words must be read as a whole and not letter-by-letter. Huey's research added ammunition to whole-word advocates and their approach began to take hold during the second quarter of this century. During the first half of the century, William S. Gray, the first president of the International Reading Association and often referred to as "the father of Dick and Jane," introduced a basal series that he probably would have considered to be a balance between phonics and a whole-word approach. However, Gray would be the first to admit he was not a fan of using explicit phonics instruction, and his basal series personified the look-say approach that dominated instruction through the early 1950s. In 1955, the pendulum swing toward whole-word instruction slowed.

In 1955, *Why Johnny Can't Read* was published. The author, Rudolph Flesch, appealed, if not to our common sense, then at least to our sense of patriotism, "There is a connection between phonics and democracy—a fundamental connection. Equal opportunity for all is one of the inalienable rights, and the word method interferes with that right" (Flesch, 1955, p. 130). While the logic of this statement is certainly weak, his impact on the general public was not. *Why Johnny Can't Read* was on most best seller lists for over thirty weeks. A close reading of *Why Johnny Can't Read* reveals an often simplistic view of the reading process. However, it was a significant step in polarizing the thinking of educators about the phonics/whole-word debate. In the mid 1960s, two important individuals in the field of reading, through their research and writing, took the debate to a higher level.

In 1967, Jeanne Chall's *Learning to Read: The Great Debate*, clearly stated that a synthetic (explicitly taught phonics) approach is superior to an analytical (whole-word) approach. Chall reviewed the significant research that had been conducted from 1910 to 1965 to reach the conclusion that systematic, explicit phonics instruction was an important component of beginning reading instruction. Interestingly, also in 1967, Kenneth Goodman, most certainly the individual most responsible for the whole language movement, published an article entitled "Reading: A Psycholinguistic Guessing Game." In this article, Goodman laid the groundwork for the concept that reading is a top-down, meaning-centered approach, where phonics is learned implicitly by students immersed in the reading and writing process. He also expressed that systematic phonics instruction was not an important component of early reading instruction. Intentionally or not, Chall and Goodman intensified the confusion and conflict regarding the function of phonics in beginning reading instruction. Over the next twenty years, the concept of reading as a top down process as supported by Goodman had greatest influence on early reading instruction. This began to change in 1985.

> **Intentionally or not, Chall and Goodman intensified the confusion and conflict regarding the function of phonics in beginning reading instruction.**

Becoming a Nation of Readers: The Report of the Commission on Reading was published in 1985. This report clearly supported the concept that reading must be meaning-centered. However, after much of the significant research on beginning reading instruction had been investigated, the following firm statement was made in *Becoming a Nation of Readers*, "The issue is no longer, as it was several decades ago, whether children should be taught phonics. The issues now are specific ones of just how it should be done" (Anderson, Hiebert, Scott, & Wilkerson, 1985, p. 37). The question, "How should it be done?" was answered this way, "When the criterion is children's year-to-year gains on standardized reading achievement tests, the available research does not permit a decisive answer, although the trend of the data favors explicit phonics" (Anderson, et. al., 1985, p. 42). While *Becoming a Nation of Readers* added support to Chall's suppositions in *Learning to Read: The Great Debate*, with its statement that children must be taught phonics, the answer to how it be taught, explicitly or implicitly, was much weaker. In 1990, stronger support to Chall's stance on the great debate was provided.

Beginning to Read: Thinking and Learning About Print (Adams, 1990), was written in conjunction with the Reading Research Center at the Center for the Study of Reading at the University of Illinois. It was supported by the Office of Educational Research and Improvement (OERI) of the United States Department of Education. Author Marilyn Jager Adams provided a comprehensive look at the research on beginning reading instruction and then took a significant step in concluding the phonics debate. She stated, in fact insisted, that the teaching of beginning reading involve phonics taught explicitly and early. Adams' book is an impressive document. It carefully examines the phonics debate, and it is persuasive in its conclusions. *Beginning to Read* is a difficult book to ignore. When examined alongside *Learning to Read: The Great Debate* and *Becoming a Nation of Readers*, it seems appropriate to view phonics as a significant component of beginning reading instruction and to also view the teaching of phonics as a viable, and perhaps preferable, instructional strategy.

Teaching students to use phonics skills should be a part of reading instruction.

Phonics: An Important Consideration

Teaching students to use phonics skills should be a part of reading instruction; however, how the skills are taught continues to be a point of concern. While the evidence leans toward teaching phonics explicitly, it is far from overwhelming. Let us re-examine the statement, "When the criterion is children's year-to-year gains on standardized reading achievement tests, the available research does not permit a decisive answer, although the trend of the data favors explicit phonics" (Anderson, et. al, 1985, p. 42). For additional consideration, couple such a statement with the following made by Chall (1967) in *Learning to Read: The Great Debate*.

> A beginning code-emphasis program will not cure all reading ills. It cannot guarantee that *all* children will learn to read easily. Nor have the results of meaning-emphasis programs been so disastrous that all academic and emotional failures can be blamed on them, as some proponents and publishers of new code-emphasis programs claim. But the evidence does show that a changeover to code-emphasis programs for the beginner can improve the situation somewhat, and in this all too imperfect world even a small improvement is worth working for. I believe that method changes, if made in the right spirit, will lead to improved reading standards (p. 309).

These statements, while supportive of the explicit teaching of phonics, are certainly not overwhelmingly powerful endorsements.

While Adams (1990) is firm in her commitment to explicit phonics instruction, she is not supportive of a bottom-up approach, the approach most often associated with explicit phonic instruction, where one skill must sequentially follow another. She makes this statement when discussing effective reading programs:

> Finally, none of these programs embodies the misguided hypothesis that reading skills are best developed from the bottom up. In the reading situation, as in any effective communication situation, the message or text provides but one of the critical sources of information. The rest must come from the readers' own prior knowledge. Further, in the reading situation as in any other learning situation, the learnability of a pattern depends critically on the prior knowledge and higher-order relationships it evokes. In both fluent reading and its acquisition, the reader's knowledge must be aroused interactively and in parallel. Neither understanding nor learning can proceed hierarchically from the bottom up. Phonological awareness, letter recognition facility, familiarity with spelling patterns, spelling-sound relations, and individual words must be developed in concert with real reading and real writing and with deliberate reflection on the forms, functions, and meanings of texts (p. 422).

There seems strong agreement that phonics be taught. There is less agreement as to how it should be taught.

What seems important to remember, as one examines the history of this great debate, is that the reading needs of students are more important than winning the debate. There seems strong agreement that phonics be taught. There is less agreement as to how it should be taught. It is hoped that the debate can be curtailed or discontinued altogether. Teachers should focus not on the debate but on students, and look to ensure that the skills of phonics are learned in meaningful ways.

Phonics: A Definition and Overview

As defined earlier, phonics is the association of sounds with symbols. Because our alphabet consists of consonants and vowels, phonics is the process of giving sounds to the letters of the alphabet. This seems a straightforward process. However, associating sounds with the letters of the alphabet can be a challenging process. Differences abound, depending on where we live, the dialect we use, and the words we are trying to read. In California, people put *oil* in their cars, while in Texas, *all* is added. Speaking of *car*, where does the "r" go when it is pronounced in and around New York City?

What is important to remember is that the sound-symbol relationship varies from word to word, from person to person, and from region to region. The authors of *Becoming a Nation of Readers* make this statement: "All that phonics can be expected to do is help children get approximate pronunciations" (p. 41). As each of us has developed a different process for the use of phonics, we need to guide our students to develop the concept that phonics is not a perfect process but one that needs to be personalized. When students realize this, they are on their way to developing their own logic of the code. For this to happen, students must be taught the most essential components of phonics very early in their reading careers. In *Becoming a Nation of Readers*, the task is stated clearly, "The right maxims for phonics are: Do it early. Keep it simple" (Anderson, et. al., 1985, p. 43).

> **What is important to remember is that the sound-symbol relationship varies from word to word, from person to person, and from region to region.**

To follow this statement, three important areas need to be examined. We will define important terms associated with phonics, look at important sound-symbol relationships, and examine the phonic generalizations, or rules, that do and do not work.

Definitions of Phonic Terms

The following terms are commonly used in relation to phonics. The definitions are ours but, in almost all cases, closely reflect common definitions found in professional literature.

◆ Vowels

The letters "a," "e," "i," "o," and "u" are always labeled vowels. The letters "y" and "w" sometimes function as vowels when at the end of words. The vowel sound is one produced by a relatively free passage of the air stream through the voice-making mechanisms.

◆ Consonants

Consonants are usually those letters that are not vowels. The consonant sound is one produced by a partial or complete obstruction of the air stream through the voice-making mechanisms. Again, the letters "y" and "w" can cause confusion. They are normally consonants at the beginnings of words and vowels at the end of words.

◆ Consonant Blends

A consonant blend is two or more consecutive consonants that work or blend together while maintaining their own sound. The "str" in *street* is an example of a blend, as is the "fl" in *flower*. Consonant blends are sometimes labeled consonant clusters.

◆ Consonant Digraphs

A consonant digraph is two consecutive consonants representing one sound. There are both regular and variant digraphs. Regular digraphs produce a single sound, unique to the two consonants involved. The "ch" in chin is a regular digraph.

Variant digraphs produce a sound associated with an existing letter of the alphabet. The "ph" in phonics, the "gh" in enough, and the "ch" in character are variant digraphs. Most digraphs, both regular and variant, have the letter "h" as the second of the two letters involved. The "ng" at the end of words such as thing is the exception.

◆ Hard "C"

The letter "c" generally produces the /k/ sound when followed by "a," "o," "u," or a consonant.

◆ Soft "C"

The letter "c" generally produces the /s/ sound when followed by "e," "i," or "y."

◆ Hard "G"

The letter "g" generally produces a /g/ sound when followed by "a," "o," "u," or a consonant.

◆ Soft "G"

The letter "g" generally produces the /j/ sound when followed by "e," "i," or "y."

◆ Long Vowels

It is generally stated that long vowels say their own name. The "a" in ape would be labeled a long vowel sound. Long vowels are sometimes called glided vowels.

◆ Short Vowels

Short vowel sounds, sometimes called unglided vowels, are the phonemes associated with the vowels in the words *at*, *egg*, *it*, *ox*, and *bum*.

◆ R-Controlled Vowels

When a vowel is followed by an "r," the vowel is generally neither long nor short but influenced by the "r." The word *car* is a good example of an r-controlled vowel.

A consonant digraph is two consecutive consonants representing one sound.

◆ Vowel Diphthongs

Diphthongs are tricky concepts. Diphthong is a Greek word which means "having two sounds." While the term diphthong can be applied to both consonants and vowels, in reading we generally talk about vowel diphthongs. A vowel diphthong is a subtle combination of two vowel sounds. The vowel combinations most often labeled diphthongs are the "oi" in *oil*, "oy" in *toy*, "ow" in *cow*, and "ou" in *out*.

◆ Vowel Digraphs

Vowel digraphs are generally defined as two consecutive vowels producing one sound. There are regular and variant forms. Regular vowel digraphs produce sounds that are long, as in the word *bead*, and variant vowel digraphs produce sounds that are not long, as in the word *bread*. The concept of regular as long and variant as not long offers students little useful information. When students see two vowels, they know they produce a single long or not long sound unless a diphthong, or a double "oo" combination is involved.

> **Diphthong is a Greek word which means "having two sounds."**

◆ Schwa

The schwa is neither a long nor a short sound. It is the sound heard in the initial letter "a" of the word *afraid*. It is typically found in the unaccented syllable of words.

Phonics: Sound/Symbol Relationships

◆ Consonant Sounds

b	bear		p	pear
c	cat		q	queen
d	dog		r	race
f	face		s	seven
g	goat		t	teacher
h	hen		v	vase
j	jug		w	wagon
k	king		x	box
l	lake		y	yellow
m	monkey		z	zebra
n	nice			

◆ Vowel Sounds

Short Sounds			Long Sounds	
a	at		a	ace
e	echo		e	eat
i	it		i	ice
o	ox		o	open
u	up		u	unicorn

◆ **Vowel + r**

far
her
dirt
more
fur

◆ **Consonants with Two or More Sounds**

c	consonant
c	city
g	got
g	gyrate
s	six
s	is
s	sure
x	xylophone
x	exist
x	box

◆ **Consonant Blends (Beginning of words)**

bl	blend	pl	place	tr	tree
br	bright	pr	pretty	tw	twenty
cl	clear	sc	score	sch	school
cr	crown	sk	sky	scr	screech
dr	drive	sl	slippery	shr	shrink
dw	dwell	sm	smell	spl	splash
fl	floor	sn	snail	spr	spring
fr	from	sp	spot	str	street
gl	glue	st	stop	thr	through
gr	grumpy	sw	swim		

◆ **Consonant Blends (End of Words)**

ld	child
mp	camp
nd	send
nt	bent
sk	risk

◆ **Consonant Digraphs**

(Regular)		(Variant)	
ch	church	ch	character
sh	ship	gh	enough
th	that	ph	phone
wh	when		

◆ **Diphthongs**

oi	oil
ou	out
ow	cow
oy	toy

If the above information sounds precise and consistent, it is important to remember that we are dealing with an imperfect system. Bryson (1990) tells us we have more than forty sounds in English and over 200 ways of spelling them. We can render the "sh" in up to fourteen ways; we can spell the long "o" and long "a" in more than a dozen ways. If we count proper nouns, the word *air* can be spelled a remarkable thirty-eight ways. We must be especially careful and consistent as we select the phonic rules or generalizations to teach students so they can be as successful as possible.

Burns, Roe, and Ross (1996) felt that students should not be inundated with rules. They examined the lists of generalizations by Bailey (1967), Burmeister (1968), Clymer (1963), and Evans (1967) and came to the conclusion that out of the multitude of rules that could be taught, the following list was sufficiently short and useful.

1. When the letters "c" and "g" are followed by "e," "i," or "y," they generally have soft sounds: the /s/ sound for the letter "c" and the /j/ sound for the letter "g." (Examples are *cent*, *city*, and *giant*.) When "c" and "g" are followed by "o," "a," or "u," they generally have hard sounds: "g" has its own sound, and "c" has the sound of /k/. (Examples are *cat*, *cut*, and *go*.)

2. When any two like consonants are next to each other, only one is sounded, as in *letter* and *butter*.

3. The letters "ch" usually has the sound heard in *church*, although it sometimes sounds like /sh/ or /k/ as in *Charlotte* and *character*.

4. When "kn" are the first two letters in a word, the "k" is not sounded, as in *knot*.

5. When "wr" are the first two letters in a word, the "w" is not sounded, as is *write*.

6. When "ck" are the last two letters in a word, the sound of the letter "k" is given, as in *truck*.

7. The sound of a vowel preceding "r" is neither long nor short, as in *car* and *far*.

8. In the vowel combinations "oa," "ee," "ai," and "ay," the first vowel is generally long and the second is not sounded, as in *boat*.

9. The double vowels "oi," "oy," and "ou" usually form diph-thongs. The "ow" combination frequently stands for the long /o/ sound, but it may also form a diphthong. (Examples are *toy*, *out*, and *cow*.)

10. If a word has one vowel and that vowel is at the end of the word, the vowel usually represents its long sound, as in *go*.

11. If a word has only one vowel and the vowel is not at the end of the word, the vowel usually represents its short sound, as in *cat*.

12. If a word has two vowels and one is the final "e," the first vowel is usually long and the final "e" is not sounded, as in *cake*.

Burns, Roe, and Ross (1996) stress that students must be guided to see that generalizations help them to derive probable pronunciations rather than infallible results.

Strategies for Developing Phonic Skills

Before a discussion on strategies for teaching phonic skills can be initiated, a decision needs to be made on the order in which the components of phonics should be taught. Below, we present the order in which we suggest the concepts be taught and then provide a justification for our choice.

1. Begin with the consonant sounds /b/, hard /c/, /d/, hard /g/, /h/, /j/, /k/, /m/, /n/, /p/, /t/, and /w/.

   We suggest these consonants first as they are most consistent. They generally represent one sound. Within these consonants, we suggest teachers do not teach the letter sounds of "b," "d," and "p" at the same time because the sounds and letter shapes are similar and can be confused. The same is true of "m," and "n." Teachers should also note that the letters "c," "g," "h," and "w" can be more difficult to learn as their letter names are distinctively different from their sounds.

2. Teach the short sounds of the five common vowels /a/, /e/, /i/, /o/, and /u/.

   It is our experience that students find learning the short vowel sounds most useful. They can blend them with the consonants presented above to read a large number of one syllable words.

3. Teach students the consonants sounds /f/, /l/, /r/, and /s/.

   We suggest waiting to teach these consonants sounds until students are comfortable with the more consistent consonants. Young students often find these sounds difficult to articulate.

It is our experience that students find learning the short vowel sounds most useful.

4. Teach the soft /c/ and the soft /g/.

   It is a good idea to separate the teaching of the hard and soft /c/ and /g/ sounds to avoid confusion on the part of students. Let students get comfortable with the hard sounds and then teach them the soft sounds.

5. Teach the long sounds of the five common vowels.

   Again, let students get comfortable with the short vowel sounds and then teach them the long vowel sounds.

6. Teach appropriate rimes and corresponding onsets.

   Examine the rimes presented in the chapter entitled Structural Analysis. Select those that include just the vowel and consonant sounds already introduced (i.e., the rime *at*, and the onsets of letters "b," "c," and "f"). Rimes are especially useful as they help students recognize familiar letter patterns and how the combinations influence the sounds that are made.

Rimes are especially useful as they help students recognize familiar letter patterns and how their combinations influence the sounds that are made.

7. Teach the consonant sounds /q/, /v/, /x/, /y/, and /z/.

   We suggest waiting to teach the sounds associated with these consonants because they are not consistent. The /q/ represents a new concept because it always works with the letter "u." We also strongly suggest that /x/ be taught in the final position of words such as *box* to avoid confusing students.

8. Teach the vowel plus "r" generalization.

   This should be taught after students become comfortable with the long and short sounds of the vowels.

9. Teach common two-letter consonant blends.

   Blends should be taught after students have mastered the individual consonant sounds.

10. Teach the consonant digraphs.

    As the majority of consonant digraphs create single new sounds, wait to introduce digraphs until after students have gained confidence in the sound/symbol process.

11. Teach common three-letter consonant blends.

    The concepts of the blending of three consonants can often be a complex concept and a difficult task for young learners. There should be no hurry to teach them.

12. Teach other sound/symbol relationships on an as-needed basis.

We feel that the sound/symbol relationships not discussed above are either too rare or inconsistent to teach to students on a systematic basis. While there are many who will argue with this, we feel that vowel digraphs, diphthongs, and other, even more esoteric generalizations, are too confusing for many young readers. Students learning the phonetic process are often hindered rather than helped by trying to learn the difference between such concepts as the voiced and unvoiced /th/. If we think back to *Becoming a Nation of Readers,* a very clear statement was made, "The right maxims for phonics are: Do it early. Keep it simple" (Anderson, et. al., 1996, p. 43). Manzo and Manzo (1995) are even more basic: "A little bit of phonics can go a long way" (p.187).

We have presented the order in which we like to teach phonics concepts. The next step is developing a process for teaching phonics skills. Cunningham, Moore, Cunningham, and Moore (1989) have developed a seven step prototype for a phonics lesson that we particularly like. The steps are listed below. A sample lesson will follow.

We have found that when students can take the sound being taught and relate it to a word already in their speaking vocabulary, the sound becomes much less abstract and more real to students.

1. Review and explain the goal of the lesson.
2. Teach auditory discrimination of the sound.
3. Teach association of letter with sound by using a known word as a key word.
4. Have students find the letter in other words and remind them that letters do not always have the same sounds.
5. Have students apply the sound to figuring out new words during the lesson.
6. Guide students in applying their new letter-sound knowledge to reading.
7. Remind students to apply the sound when reading on their own.

The following presents an example of a phonics lesson that uses, with some modification, these seven steps. We feel that step three is a key component of the lesson. We have found that when students can take the sound being taught and relate it to a word already in their speaking vocabulary, the sound becomes much less abstract and more real to them. In this lesson, we focus on the short /e/ sound.

1. Today we are going to learn another vowel sound. Do you remember the short vowel sound for the letter "a ?" Do you remember the key word for this sound? (Write *apple* and "a" on the board to help students remember.) Today we will learn

the short sound for the letter "e" and come up with a key word for the sound.

2. The short vowel sound in the letter "e" is the sound /e/. I hear the sound /e/ at the beginning of these words: *Ed*, *edge*, and *echo*. I am going to say some more words. Listen to see if they begin with the same sound as *Ed*. If they do, make a smile on your face. If they do not, make a frown. (Say the words *effort*, *escape*, *art*, *apple*, and *etch*. Watch for students' responses. Continue until you are sure students are comfortable hearing the difference between the short /e/ and other beginning vowel sounds.)

3. I have said a lot of words that begin with the short /e/ sound. I want you to pick the word you think best makes that sound. The word can have the sound at its beginning, middle, or end. Have students nominate words and tell why they like them. (Write their suggestions on the board. Have the class vote on the word they feel is the best key word. Have the student whose word is selected wear a card for the rest of the day with the word printed on it and the letter with the short /e/ underlined. Designate him or her the "Short /e/ Expert" for the class.)

4. Remember yesterday I read you a story called *The Little Red Hen* (Galdone, 1973)? I am going to read it again. Listen and see if you hear the short /e/ sound in some of the words in the story. (Read the story to the students and slightly emphasize words with the short /e/ sound.) Now, I am going to write its title on the board. (Write the title, *The Little Red Hen*, on the board.) Who can come up and underline each letter "e?" (Once each letter is underlined, have students decide if the letter underlined has the same sound as it has in the chosen key word. Remind students that the letter "e" does not always make the short /e/ sound heard in the key word and that sometimes you hear the sound in the middle or at the end of words.)

5. (Ask students what the sound of /e/ is in the key word. Write the word *set* on the board. Ask students what sound the letter "s" makes and what sound the letter "t" makes. Place your hand under the "s" and have them say the sound, then under the "e" and have them say the sound, then under the "t" and have them say the sound.) Now I am going to say the same sounds and blend them all together. What is the word I am saying when the sounds are blended together? (Continue this process with three letter words having familiar consonants and the short /e/ sound until students are reasonably successful.)

6. Now we are going to read a story that has some new words with letter "e." When you see these words, try the short /e/ sound that you hear in our key word. Remember, the "e" will not always make the short /e/ sound. Try the sound and see if you can come up with a word that makes sense in the story. Read the story until you come to a word with a short /e/ sound. (Guide students through sounding out the word. Do this until students are comfortable with the process. Then let them read on their own.)

7. We have learned a new sound today. What was it? (Ask students what the key word is for the sound.) When we see a word with the letter "e" in it, will it always make the short /e/ sound we hear in the key word? As you are reading today, see if you can use the short /e/ sound to help you read new words.

Vowel sounds are often difficult for students to learn. When students are introduced to them in a rich variety of settings, the sounds become easier to understand. The lesson that follows is an effective example for teaching the short vowel sound /a/.

Vowel sounds are often difficult for students to learn.

Phonics Skills in Context: Short "A"

Book: *The Cat in the Hat*
Author: Dr. Seuss
Publisher: Random House, New York, 1967
Summary: The classic, rhyming story of the cat in the hat who entertains two small children for the day.
Recommended Grade Level: K–2
Related Poetry: "Anteater" by Shel Silverstein, *A Light in the Attic* (HarperCollins, New York, 1981).

Skill Activity

Students listen for short "a" words in the story. Then they create their own "Cat in the Hat" paper bag hats and decorate them with short "a" pictures.

Materials

- grocery-size paper bags
- picture cards
- glue
- word cards (page 40)
- crayons or markers
- chart paper • scissors

Lesson

Introduce the Literature: Show students the cover and ask how many of them have heard the story before.

Read the Literature: Read the literature selection. Allow time for discussion.

Introduce the Skill Lesson:

1. Have students listen for the short "a" sound as you read the title of the book. Then, ask students for other short "a" words and add to chart paper to use as a word bank.
2. Hold up the word cards one at a time for children to read. Pass out cards to students or small groups. As you read the story, ask them to hold up the cards when the word is read.
3. Allow students to make their own hats by rolling up the bottom of a paper bag (to form the brim) and turning the bag upside down.
4. Have students color and cut out the short "a" picture cards. Glue them to the hat.

Learning Center Activity: Have students make cats. Students can use crayons to decorate their cats. Have students paint over their cats with a wash of diluted paint or food coloring.

Cooperative Learning Activity: Have students brainstorm and write short "a" words on a hat pattern.

Across the Curriculum: Physical Education

Have students do an aerobic workout or some acrobatics.

Reprinted from TCM 791 Teaching Basic Skills Through Literature: Phonics, *Teacher Created Materials, 1995*

Extension Activities

Movement Activities
Stress the short "a" sound as students participate in the following movements: ant crawl, alligator crawl, swing an ax, follow after, breathe air, and run like an antelope.

Multisensory Activity
On 6" x 8" (15 cm x 20 cm) tagboard, have children paste capital and lowercase "a's" from magazines onto an upper and lowercase "a."

Creative Writing
Have students complete this story starter: "I planted an apple seed in my garden, but instead of an apple tree, up came ..." Provide blank apple shape patterns for students to complete. Attach student pages to the cover and the first page.

Handwriting
On 12" by 18" (30 cm x 46 cm) lined newsprint, ask children to copy this sentence: "A is for apple, ant (make thumbprints), alphabet, and antler."

Cooking

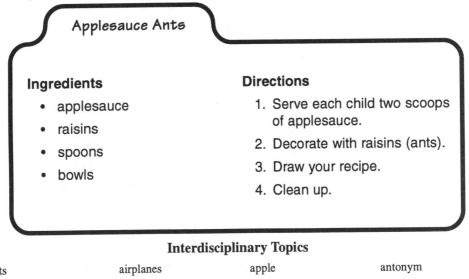

Applesauce Ants

Ingredients
- applesauce
- raisins
- spoons
- bowls

Directions
1. Serve each child two scoops of applesauce.
2. Decorate with raisins (ants).
3. Draw your recipe.
4. Clean up.

Interdisciplinary Topics

ants	airplanes	apple	antonym
animals	Africa	antelope	adverb
amphibian	Alaska	Aztec Indians	adjective
Arbor Day	air	Antarctic	Alabama
astronauts	address	alligator	acid rain

Reprinted from TCM 791 Teaching Basic Skills Through Literature: Phonics, *Teacher Created Materials, 1995*

Short "A" Word Cards

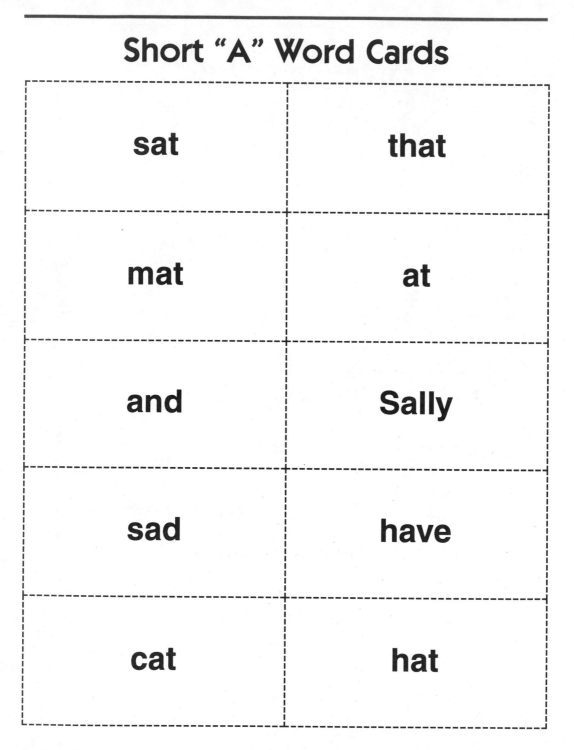

sat	that
mat	at
and	Sally
sad	have
cat	hat

Reprinted from TCM 791 Teaching Basic Skills Through Literature: Phonics, *Teacher Created Materials, 1995*

Children's Books that Feature Specific Sounds

We have featured good children's literature for every component of the decoding process. This section on phonics is no different. As a sound is introduced, literature that features that sound should be read to the students. This shows the students two important things. First, that good literature is full of familiar sounds. Second, students who learn their sounds will, eventually, be able to read many of the books that have been read to them. Additional titles can be found in *Teaching Basic Skills Through Literature* (Ryan, 1995).

◆ **Short /a/**

Anno, Mitsumasa	*Anno's Alphabet* (1975, Harper & Row)
Carratello, Patty	*My Cap* (1988, Teacher Created Materials)
Flack, Marjorie	*Angus and the Cat* (1989, Doubleday)
Gag, Wanda	*Millions of Cats* (1977, Putnam)
Griffith, Hellen	*Alex and the Cat* (1982, Greenwillow)
Most, Bernard	*There's an Ant in Anthony* (1992, Morrow)
Nodset, Joan	*Who Took the Farmer's Hat?* (1963, HarperCollins)
Robins, Joan	*Addie Meets Max* (1985, HarperCollins)
Schmidt, Karen	*The Gingerbread Man* (1985, Scholastic)
Seuss, Dr.	*The Cat in the Hat* (1987, Random)
Seuss, Dr.	*The Cat in the Hat Comes Back* (1988, Random)

◆ **Long /a/**

Aardema, Verna	*Bringing the Rain to Kapiti Plain* (1981, Dial)
Bang, Molly	*The Paper Crane* (1985, Greenwillow)
Blume, Judy	*The Pain and the Great One* (1984, Macmillan)
Burton, Virginia Lee	*Katy & the Big Snow* (1976, Houghton Mifflin)
Carratello, Patty	*Skate, Kate, Skate!* (1988, Teacher Created Materials)

> As a sound is introduced, literature that features that sound should be read to the students.

41

Henkes, Kevin	*Sheila Rae, the Brave* (1988, Puffin)
Howard, Elizabeth Fitzgerald	*The Train to Lulu's* (1988, Macmillan)
McPhail, David	*The Train* (1977, Little, Brown)

◆ **Short and Long /a/**

Aliki	*Jack and Jake* (1986, Greenwillow)
Slobodkina, Esphyr	*Caps for Sale* (1947, HarperCollins)

◆ **Short /e/**

Carratello, Patty	*Brett, My Pet* (1988, Teacher Created Materials)
Demi	*The Empty Pot* (1990, Holt)
Galdone, Paul	*The Little Red Hen* (1987, Houghton Mifflin)

◆ **Long /e/**

Archambault, John	*Counting Sheep* (1989, Holt)
Keller, Holly	*Ten Sleepy Sheep* (1983, Greenwillow)
Martin, Bill	*Brown Bear, Brown Bear, What Do You See?* (1983, Holt)
Oppenheim, Joanne	*Have You Seen Trees?* (1995, Scholastic)
Wellington, Monica	*The Sheep Follow* (1992, Dutton)

◆ **Short /i/**

Browne, Anthony	*Willy the Wimp* (1989, Knopf)
Carratello, Patty	*Will Bill?* (1988, Teacher Created Materials)
Ets, Marie Hall	*Gilberto and the Wind* (1963, Viking)
Hutchkins, Pat	*Titch* (1993, Macmillan)
Keats, Ezra Jack	*Whistle for Willie* (1977, Puffin)
Lionni, Leo	*Swimmy* (1963, Knopf)
Lobel, Arnold	*Small Pig* (1988, HarperCollins)
McPhail, David	*Fix-It* (1993, Puffin)

◆ **Long /i/**

Waber, Bernard	*Ira Sleeps Over* (1993, Houghton Mifflin)

Berenstain, Stan and Jan	*The Bike Lesson* (1994, Random House)
Carratello, Patty	*Mice on Ice* (1988, Teacher Created Materials)
Carlson, Nancy	*I Like Me* (1988, Puffin)
Cole, Sheila	*When the Tide is Low* (1985, Lothrop)
Hazen, Barbara S.	*Tight Times* (1983, Puffin)

◆ **Short /o/**

Benchley, Nathaniel	*Oscar Otter* (1980, HarperCollins)
Carratello, Patty	*Dot's Pot* (1988, Teacher Created Materials)
Crews, Donald	*Ten Black Dots* (1986, Greenwillow)
Dunrea, Olivier	*Mogwogs on the March* (1985, Holiday)
Emberley, Barbara	*Drummer Hoff* (1985, Simon and Schuster)
McKissack, Patricia C.	*Flossie and the Fox* (1986, Dial)
Seuss, Dr.	*Fox in Socks* (1965, Random)
Seuss, Dr.	*Hop on Pop* (1987, Random)

◆ **Long /o/**

Carratello, Patty	*My Old Gold Boat* (1988, Teacher Created Materials)
Cole, Brock	*The Giant's Toe* (1986, Farrar, Straus, & Giroux)
Gerstein, Mordicai	*Roll Over!* (1988, Crown)
Johnston, Tony	*The Adventures of Mole and Troll* (1989, Dell)
Johnston, Tony	*Night Noises and Other Mole and Troll Stories* (1989, Dell)
Langstaff, John	*Oh, A Hunting We Will Go* (1987, Macmillan)
Shulevitz, Uri	*One Monday Morning* (1986, Macmillan)
Tresselt, Alvin	*White Snow, Bright Snow* (1989, Lothrop)

◆ **Short /u/**

| Carratello, Patty | *My Truck and My Pup* (1988, Teacher Created Materials) |

Carroll, Ruth	*Where's the Bunny?* (1992, Kids Books)
Feczko, Kathy	*Umbrella Parade* (1985, Troll)
Marshall, James	*The Cut-Ups* (1986, Puffin)
Udry, Janice May	*Thump and Plunk* (1981, HarperCollins)
Yashima, Taro	*Umbrella* (1977, Puffin)

◆ **Long /u/**

Carratello, Patty	*Duke the Blue Mule* (1988, Teacher Created Materials)
Correlle, Bruce & Katharine	*Sarah's Unicorn* (1985, HarperCollins)
McCloskey, Robert	*Blueberries for Sal* (1988, Viking Press)
Segal, Lore	*Tell Me a Trudy* (1989, Farrar, Straus, & Giroux)

◆ **Short Vowels a-e-i-o-u**

Carratello, Patty	*This is Fred* (1988, Teacher Created Materials)

◆ **Long Vowels a-e-i-o-u**

Carratello, Patty	*Gail's Paint Pail* (1988, Teacher Created Materials)

◆ **Letter "B"**

Brett, Jan	*Goldilocks and the Three Bears* (1990, Putnam)
Cohen, Miriam	*Best Friends* (1989, Macmillan)
Martin, Jr. Bill	*Brown Bear, Brown Bear* (1983, Holt)

◆ **Letter "C"**

Freeman, Don	*A Pocket for Corduroy* (1989, Puffin)
Gag, Wanda	*Millions of Cats* (1977, Putnam)
Rae, H A.	*Curious George* (1994, Houghton Mifflin)

◆ **Letter "D"**

Gibbons, Gail	*Dinosaurs, Dragonflies, and Diamonds* (1988, Macmillan)
McCloskey, Robert	*Make Way for Ducklings* (1993, Putnam)

◆ Letter "F"

Lionni, Leo	*Frederick* (1966, Pantheon Books)
Oxenbury, Helen	*Friends* (1990, Greenwillow)
Palmer, Helen	*A Fish Out of Water* (1961, Beginner)
Pfister, Marcus	*The Rainbow Fish* (1992, North-South Books)

◆ Letter "G"

Brown, Margaret Wise	*Goodnight Moon* (1993, Scholastic)
Carle, Eric	*The Grouchy Ladybug* (1977, Harper & Row)
Ehlert, Lois	*Growing Vegetable Soup* (1991, Harcourt, Brace, & Jovanovich)

◆ Letter "H"

Barton, Byron	*Building a House* (1992, Hampton-Brown)
Hoberman, Mary Ann	*A House is a House for Me* (1993, Puffin)
Morris, Ann	*Houses and Homes* (1995, Morrow)

◆ Letter "J"

Arnold, Ted	*No Jumping on the Bed* (1987, Dial)
Walsh, Helen Stoll	*Hop Jump* (1993, Harcourt)

◆ Letter "K"

Payne, Emmy	*Katy No-Pocket* (1973, Houghton Mifflin)
Yashima, Mitsu & Taro	*Momo's Kitten* (1977, Puffin)

◆ Letter "L"

Waber, Bernard	*Lyle, Lyle, Crocodile* (1987, Houghton Mifflin)

◆ Letter "M"

Brown, Margaret Wise	*Goodnight Moon* (1993, Scholastic)
Brown, Margaret Wise	*Wait Till the Moon Is Full* (1989, HarperCollins)

◆ Letter "N"

Arnold, Ted	*No Jumping on the Bed* (1987, Dial)
Mayer, Mercer	*There's Something in My Attic* (1992, Puffin)
Wood, Audrey	*The Napping House* (1991, Harcourt)

◆ Letter "P"

Carle, Eric	*Pancakes, Pancakes* (1970, Alfred A. Knopf)
Pizer, Abigail	*It's a Perfect Day* (1992, HarperCollins)
Wood, Audrey	*Little Penguin's Tale* (1993, Harcourt)

◆ Letter "Q"

Brown, Margaret Wise	*The Quiet Noisy Book* (1993, HarperCollins)
Carle, Eric	*The Very Quiet Cricket* (1990, Putnam)

◆ Letter "R"

Brown, Margaret Wise	*The Runaway Bunny* (1985 HarperCollins)
Hutchins, Pat	*Rose's Walk* (1971, Macmillan)
Pfister, Marcus	*The Rainbow Fish* (1992, North-South Books)

◆ Letter "S"

Lionni, Leo	*Swimmy* (1963, Knopf)
Steig, William	*Sylvester and the Magic Pebble* (1988, Simon & Schuster)

◆ Letter "T"

Baker, Alan	*Two Tiny Mice* (1991, Dial)
Lester, Helen	*Tacky the Penguin* (1990, Houghton Mifflin)
Weiss, Leslie	*My Teacher Sleeps in School* (1985, Puffin)

◆ Letter "V"

Andrews, Jan	*Very Last First Time* (1986, Macmillan)

Carle, Eric	*The Very Hungry Caterpillar* (1986, Putnam)
Carle, Eric	*The Very Busy Spider* (1989, Putnam)

◆ Letter "W"

Hutchins, Pat	*The Wind Blew* (1993, Macmillan)
Kantrowitz, Mildred	Willy Bear (1989, Macmillan)
Sendak, Maurice	*Where the Wild Things Are* (1988, HarperCollins)

◆ Letter "X"

Fox, Mem	*Hattie and the Fox* (1992, Macmillan)
Hall, Donald	*Ox-Cart Man* (1983, Puffin)

◆ Letter "Y"

Grey, Judith	*Yummy, Yummy* (1981, Troll)
Lionni, Leo	*Little Blue and Little Yellow* (1994, Morrow)

◆ Letter "Z"

McDermott, Gerald	*Zomo the Rabbit* (1992, Harcourt)
Peet, Bill	*Zella, Zack, and Zodiac* (1989, Houghton Mifflin)

◆ "Ch" Digraph

Martin, Bill, Jr. & Archambault, John	*Chicka Chicka Boom Boom* (1989, Simon & Schuster)
Williams, Vera	*A Chair for My Mother* (1994, Morrow)

◆ "Th" Digraph

Emberley, Rebecca	*Three Cool Kids* (1995, Little, Brown)
Tashjian, Virginia	*Juba This and Juba That* (1995, Little, Brown)

◆ "Wh" Digraph

Gerson, Mary-Joan	*Why the Sky Is Far Away* (1992, Little, Brown)
Godkin, Celia	*What About Ladybugs?* (1995, Sierra Club)

The books presented above are primarily those we read to students. However, most teachers ask, "What are the types of books students should read as part of their early reading experiences?" *Becoming a Nation of Readers* makes this statement:

The important point is that a high proportion of the words in the earliest selections children read should conform to the phonics they have already been taught. Otherwise they will not have enough opportunity to practice, extend, and refine their knowledge of letter-sound relationships (Anderson, et. al., 1985, p. 47).

We also suggest that these books only contain words in students' speaking vocabularies. When this is the case, students can validate when they are using phonics correctly. In the list of books above, there were several developed by Teacher Created Materials and written by Patty Carratello that do an excellent job of presenting words to students with consistent letter-sound relationships.

Concluding Remarks

Teaching phonic skills to students is a viable instructional process; however, it certainly is not a perfect process. The sound-symbol relationship in the English language simply is not very regular. Fortunately, it does not have to be. Groff (1986) found that beginning readers can achieve reasonable approximations of words through the use of phonics skills. Generally, these approximations are close enough to words in students' speaking vocabularies to allow them to infer a successful pronunciation. Phonics can be especially productive when it is used in conjunction with structural analysis, the focus of the next chapter.

Teaching phonic skills to students is a viable instructional process; however, it certainly is not a perfect process.

48

Structural Analysis

What is structural analysis?

Structural analysis is an often neglected component of decoding instruction. And, if it is introduced, it is generally in the third grade or later. We strongly suggest that structural analysis be a significant component of instruction and that it be introduced as an initial part of the decoding process. One reason for this centers around our broad and simple definition of structural analysis. We define it as the process students use to analyze the structure of a word. When students look at the components of a compound word, become aware of affixes, or look for familiar "chunks" in words, we feel they are using the process of structural analysis. The process of structural analysis is an important tool for students when they begin to encounter multi-syllabic words. Phonics can work reasonably well with one syllable words but quickly becomes unwieldy with longer words. Let us examine, just for fun, a word unfamiliar to many adults. The word is *pusillanimous*. Obviously, this word cannot be decoded by sounding out each letter in order. What most do is compare *pusillanimous* with words, or parts of words (chunks), already known. The "pu" begins like *pupil*, the "sill" is a familiar part, and the "animous" is found in *unanimous*. While this is not a perfect process—*father* can quickly become *fat her*, for example—

> **Structural analysis is an often neglected component of decoding instruction.**

49

it is more viable than trying to teach students a firm set of rules for dividing words into syllables. Adams (1990) concurs, stating, "We can specify no fixed and final set of letter-based rules about how the mind will divide a word into syllables" (p. 122).

We are firmly committed to the concept of compare/contrast or "chunking" and find much support for the process in the literature (Adams, 1990; Cunningham, et al., 1989; Gaskins, Gaskins, & Gaskins, 1991; Gunning, 1995; Manzo & Manzo, 1995; Stahl, 1992). We are also firmly committed to introducing this concept to students early and feel one of the best ways to do so is through the process of onset and rime. Onset is the part of the word that comes before the vowel and rime is the rest of the word. Guiding students to become aware of rimes allows students to see that the relationship letters have to each other can strongly influence how they are pronounced. Becoming aware of rimes and larger word chunks frees many students from the more laborious sound/symbol process. Students are often thrilled to discover that once *at* is learned, the adding of a variety of already known consonant sounds allows them to read an amazing number of words. In this light, the 37 rimes introduced below allow students to derive nearly 500 primary-level words (Wylie & Durrell, 1970).

> **Guiding students to become aware of rimes allows students to see that the relationship letters have to each other can strongly influence how they are pronounced.**

ack	at	ide	ock
ain	ate	ight	oke
ake	aw	ill	op
ale	ay	in	or
all	eat	ine	ore
ame	ell	ing	uck
an	est	ink	ug
ank	ice	ip	ump
ap	ick	ir	unk
ash			

Strategies for teaching students to use onset and rime, as well as the broader processes of compare/contrast, chunking, or word building will now be discussed.

Strategies for Developing Structural Analysis Skills

There are two strategies worth presenting. The first, labeled "word building" by Gunning (1995) introduces students to the concept of onset and rime. The second, chunking or compare/contrast, (Cunningham, et al., 1989) takes students through a more sophisticated structural analysis process. A close examination of both processes will show that they are variations of the same concept.

Word building is a process where students are shown how to use phonetic elements to decode difficult words. Gunning gives this example:

"For instance, after being taught the -at pattern, a student who is having difficulty decoding the word *pat* is asked to see if there is any part of the word he or she can say. If necessary, the teacher might cover up the "p" so that the student can focus on *at*. The approach also works with multi-syllabic words. However, in words like *chatter* the student may have to pronounce two word parts: *at* and *er*. Usually, constructing the first part of the word triggers the pronunciation of the entire word" (Gunning, 1995, p. 487).

Cunningham, et al. (1989) present how using the process of chunking or compare/contrast can assist students in dealing with more sophisticated multi-syllabic words. They describe a lesson that guides students to see that a word like *entertainment* can be decoded by comparing chunks in it to chunks in words they already know.

Word building is a process where students are shown how to use phonetic elements to decode difficult words.

"This is a long word, but it is not a very hard word to figure out if you use some of the other words you know. *Cover all but **enter**.* The first chunk is a word you know. The second chunk you know from words like **maintain** and **contain**. *On the board, underline the **tain**.* Finally, you know the last chunk if you know *argument* or *moment*. *Write **argument** and **moment** on the board, underlining the **ment**.*" (Cunningham, et. al., 1989, p. 70).

The authors go on to say that we must remind students that if they use the probable sound of letters and the sense of what they are reading, they can figure out many more words than if they just pay attention to one of the items—letter sounds or what makes sense.

Children's Books That Feature Rimes

The following books feature various rimes. As in all our literature selections, they are to be read to students to help them become familiar with the concepts being taught. Once these books are read to students, teachers should not be surprised to see students picking them up and reading them independently.

Carratello, P.	*Skate, Kate, Skate!* (1988, Teacher Created Materials)
Carratello, P.	*Will Bill?* (1996, Teacher Created Materials)
Hennessy, B.	*Jake Baked a Cake* (1990, Viking)

Henrietta	*A Mouse in the House* (1991, Dorling Kindersley)
Seuss, Dr.	*Hop on Pop* (1987, Random House)
Seuss, Dr.	*The Cat in the Hat* (1987, Random House)
Wildsmith, B.	*The Cat Sat on a Mat* (1994, Houghton Mifflin)

Concluding Remarks

Structural analysis is a robust companion to phonics. It supplies students with a tool, when used in tandem with phonics, that allows readers to decode longer single-syllable and multi-syllabic words. Unfortunately, not all words can be sounded out, not even using the combined tools of phonics and structural analysis. This leads us to look at sight words, the topic of the next chapter.

Sight Words

A Look Ahead

In this chapter, sight words will be defined, their importance presented, and strategies for teaching them introduced. In addition, two lists of important sight words will be given.

Definition

Sight words are words that are recognized immediately without need of analysis. They are important for at least four reasons.

Sight words are words that are recognized immediately without need of analysis.

1. When students recognize words immediately, they find it easier to focus on the meaning of what is being read. Analyzing unfamiliar words takes time, equanimity, fortitude, and often tenacity. Note: If you found yourself dealing with the word *equanimity*, how to pronounce it and what it means, you may have also found yourself losing sight of the meaning of the sentence or selection. Your reading was less fluent and comprehension was less automatic.

2. Many of the highest utility words in the English language cannot be sounded out. They are irregularly spelled words and should be recognized by sight.

3. Having a rich sight vocabulary gives students a good foundation for using strategies such as compare and contrast. Once students can read *cat*, they quickly recognize the similarity to *fat*, *sat*, and *mat*.

4. Having a rich sight vocabulary gives students a good foundation for using phonics. For example, once students recognize the words *dime*, *kite*, *cake*, and *ride*, they begin to recognize a pattern that helps them identify long vowel sounds in other words, as well.

It is important to remember that the focus of reading is comprehension. Teaching sight words is an important task, as long as students understand the meaning or use of the words they are learning. Because of this fact, attention must be given to both structure words and function words.

Structure Words

Structure words are those words that have little meaning of their own. Their purpose is to maintain the structure of the sentence. Words such as *was*, *is*, and *the* are classic examples. Students find these words at best unexciting and at worst difficult to learn. Structure words should be presented in isolation as little as possible. They make most sense in context where they help hold function words together.

Function Words

Function words have importance in students' eyes. They usually have meaning even when out of context. Words such as *teacher*, *student*, *dinosaur*, and *paycheck* are all function words with rich meaning. Examples such as our more derogatory four letter forms of expression (We are talking about words that are, hopefully, seldom heard in the classroom!) are rarely forgotten by students, even when encountered only once. On a more positive note, an individual's name is an even more valuable function word.

While function words do not normally need context to give them meaning, there are two types that must have context. Homonyms and homographs are function words that need context to give them appropriate meaning. Homonyms are words spelled and pronounced the same way but with different meanings. Homographs are words spelled the same way but with different meanings and pronunciation.

The following two sentences show examples of homonyms. In these sentences, context supplies meaning.

Please *hand* me the text with the definition of a diphthong in it.

I now hold the diphthong-defining text in my *hand*.

The following sentences show examples of homographs. It is easy to see how context supplies both meaning and pronunciation.

Let me *read* the diphthong-defining text.

I *read* the diphthong-defining text.

Homophones, another form of function words, are words pronounced the same way, are usually spelled differently, and have different meanings. The meanings of homophones becomes more obvious when placed in context.

Let me tell you a *tale* about why a dog has a *tail*.

It is obvious sight words are important. However, what are the important sight words? The next section supplies some answers.

Sight Word Lists

There is a common group of words that are of high utility for readers and writers. If students can learn the 100 words presented as making up 50% of all written material, they will have a significant foundation as they involve themselves in the decoding process.

The following page has a compilation of high frequency word lists. It was developed by comparing the lists of Carroll, Davies, and Richman (1971), Fry (1980), and Eeds (1985). The words chosen are those that can be located on at least two of the three lists. They are presented in approximate order of use. To be selected for the fifty words of highest frequency, the word must have appeared on all three lists. If students can learn the first ten words, they will know approximately twenty-five percent of the words they will encounter when reading. If students learn all 100 words, they will know approximately fifty percent of the words they will encounter when reading.

There is a common group of words that are of high utility for readers and writers.

1.	the	34.	had	67.	them
2.	and	35.	as	68.	many
3.	a	36.	will	69.	see
4.	to	37.	on	70.	like
5.	in	38.	up	71.	these
6.	you	39.	out	72.	me
7.	of	40.	there	73.	words
8.	it	41.	do	74.	into
9.	is	42.	from	75.	use
10.	he	43.	were	76.	has
11.	that	44.	so	77.	way
12.	was	45.	her	78.	bike
13.	for	46.	by	79.	make
14.	I	47.	if	80.	did
15.	his	48.	their	81.	could
16.	they	49.	some	82.	more
17.	with	50.	then	83.	two
18.	are	51.	him	84.	day
19.	be	52.	us	85.	will
20.	but	53.	an	86.	come
21.	at	54.	or	87.	get
22.	one	55.	no	88.	down
23.	said	56.	my	89.	now
24.	all	57.	which	90.	little
25.	have	58.	would	91.	than
26.	what	59.	each	92.	too
27.	we	60.	how	93.	first
28.	can	61.	do	94.	been
29.	this	62.	go	95.	who
30.	not	63.	about	96.	people
31.	she	64.	could	97.	its
32.	your	65.	time	98.	water
33.	when	66.	look	99.	long
				100.	find

Eeds (1985) provides a list of books which contain a high percentage of her "bookwords." A portion of the list is provided. It begins with books that have the fewest number of different words. For example, *Snake In, Snake Out* has 38 running words, but there is a total of only eight different words in the book. In most cases, earlier listed books are easier to read than those listed later. As students read these books, they encounter and practice high utility words on a regular basis.

Author	Title	Total Words	Different Words

Author	Title	Total Words	Different Words
Bancheck, Linda. *Snake In, Snake out* (1992, Dell)		38	8
Barton, Byron. *Where's Al?* (1989, Houghton Mifflin)		34	18
Ginsberg, Mirra. *The Chick and the Duckling* (1988, Macmillan)		112	30
Burningham, John. *The Blanket* (1994, Candlewick)		66	33
Burningham, John. *The Friend* (1994, Candlewick)		51	34
Burningham, John. *The Dog* (1994, Candlewick)		69	48
Kraus, Robert. *Whose Mouse are You?* (1986, Macmillan)		108	54
Alexander, Martha. *Blackboard Bear* (1988, Dial)		128	62
dePaola, Tomie. *The Knight and the Dragon* (1992, Putnam)		129	65
Kraus, Robert. *Leo the Late Bloomer* (1994, HarperCollins)		66	70
Breinburg, Petronella. *Shawn Goes to School* (1974, HarperCollins)		132	75
Mayer, Mercer. *There's a Nightmare in My Closet* (1992, Puffin)		142	76
Buckley, Helen. *Grandfather and I* (1994, Lothrop)		291	79
Bornstein, Ruth. *Little Gorilla* (1996, Houghton Mifflin)		173	80
Brown, Margaret Wise. *The Runaway Bunny* (1985, Live Oak Media)		441	83
Burningham, John. *Mr. Grumpy's Outing* (1990, Holt)		289	95
Wells, Rosemary. *Noisy Nora* (1981, Dial)		206	101
Hutchins, Pat. *The Surprise Party* (1991, Macmillan)		336	101
Udry, Janice. *Let's Be Enemies* (1993, HarperCollins)		229	102
Clifton, Lucille. *Everett Anderson's Goodbye* (1988, Holt)		200	104

Brandenburg, Fritz. *I Wish I Was Sick Too* (1990, Morrow)	327	107
Alexander, Martha. *Move Over, Twerp* (1989, Dial)	245	107
Kellogg, Steven. *Pinkerton Behave* (1982, Dial)	233	116
Flack, Marjorie. *Ask Mr. Bear* (1990, Live Oak Media)	632	118
Lionni, Leo. *Little Blue and Little Yellow* (1994, Morrow)	284	123
Griffith, Helen. *Mine Will Said John* (1992, Greenwillow)	506	124
Sendak, Maurice. *Where the Wild Things Are* (1992, HarperCollins)	350	129
Keats, Erza Jack. *Goggles!* (1987, Macmillan)	336	139
Allard, Harry & Marshall, James. *The Stupids Die* (1985, Houghton Mifflin)	296	140
Hoban, Russell & Lillian. *The Stone Doll of Sister Brute* (1992, Dell)	494	143
Keats, Erza Jack. *Whistle for Willie* (1977, Puffin)	391	149
Asch, Frank. *Sand Cake* (1993, Gareth Stevens)	443	153
Delton, Judy. *New Girl at School* (1979, Dutton)	379	158
Burningham, John. *Avocado Baby* (1994, HarperCollins)	373	160
Allard, Harry. *The Stupids Step Out* (1993, Houghton Mifflin)	413	176
Cohen, Miriam. *Will I Have a Friend?* (1989, Macmillan)	464	277
Marshall, James. *George and Martha* (1993, Houghton Mifflin)	645	210

More importantly, sight words need to be placed in meaningful context whenever possible.

There seems little doubt that sight words are important to the decoding process. Equally important are effective instructional procedures for helping students learn them.

Sight Word Instructional Strategies

Some drill is necessary in teaching sight words. However, whenever possible, this drill needs to be fun and in the form of a game. More importantly, sight words need to be placed in meaningful context. Having students use sight words in meaningful ways in their writing is a powerful technique for having students personalize sight words. In this light, it is suggested that once students master specific sight words, the words should be added to each student's personal dictionary. These words can then be used in their writing. This is a simple, yet powerful technique for making sight words personally valuable for students.

A second technique is that of placing selected sight words on the wall around the door that students use to exit the classroom. We suggest that no more than ten words be used. On the first day, the words are placed on the wall. Students have to read at least one word before they can go out the door. On the second day, two words are read, etc. Each student can read the same word or words as read by the student immediately preceding him or her. In this way, students see and hear sight words on a repeated basis. We have found that the words should be placed in a different location around the door every two to three days so that students remember words by their appearance rather than their location. Speaking of location, words can be placed around the pencil sharpener, athletic equipment, or any other appropriate location. To use the sharpener or get a soccer ball, students must read "x" number of words.

We also like to introduce sight words that focus on important events.

We also like to introduce sight words that focus on important events. The following strategy is a fine example of how this might be done. Children can make their own short story books. They will enjoy reading these together as a class and on their own.

Making Little Books

My Little Book
of
Is It Christmas Yet?

_____

Name

One day I found a Christmas card.
"Mama! Mama!" I said,
"Is it Christmas yet?"
"Not yet," said Mama.
So I put it in the closet, and I waited.

1

Reprinted from TCM 019 Early Childhood Units for Holidays, _Teacher Created Materials, 1992_

Making Little Books *(cont.)*

One day I found a candy cane.
"Mama! Mama!" I said,
"Is it Christmas yet?"
"Not yet," said Mama.
So I put it in the closet, and I waited.   **2**

One day I found a Christmas present.
"Mama! Mama!" I said,
"Is it Christmas yet?"
"Not yet," said Mama.
So I put it in the closet, and I waited.   **3**

Reprinted from TCM 019 Early Childhood Units for Holidays, *Teacher Created Materials, 1992*

Making Little Books *(cont.)*

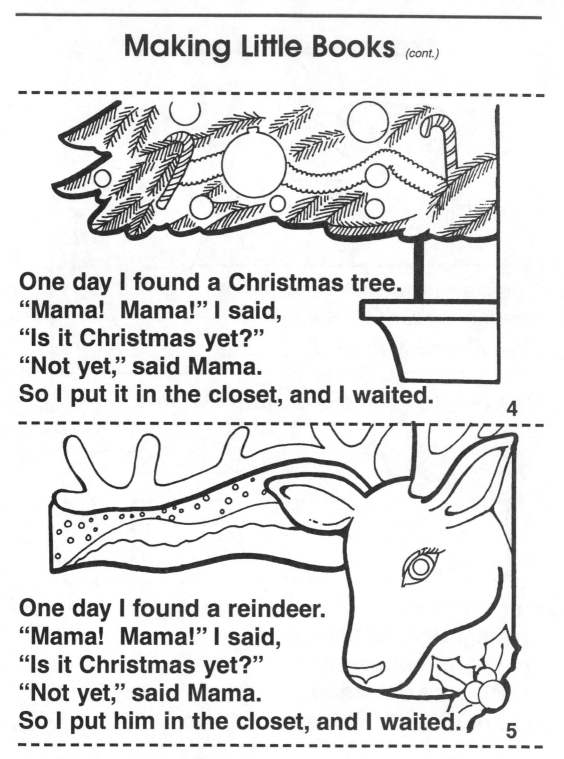

One day I found a Christmas tree.
"Mama! Mama!" I said,
"Is it Christmas yet?"
"Not yet," said Mama.
So I put it in the closet, and I waited.

4

One day I found a reindeer.
"Mama! Mama!" I said,
"Is it Christmas yet?"
"Not yet," said Mama.
So I put him in the closet, and I waited.

5

Reprinted from TCM 019 Early Childhood Units for Holidays, *Teacher Created Materials, 1992*

Making Little Books *(cont.)*

One day I found an elf.
"Mama! Mama!" I said,
"Is it Christmas yet?"
"Not yet," said Mama.
So I put him in the closet, and I waited.   6

One day I found Santa!
"Mama! Mama!" I said,
"Is it Christmas yet?"
"Yes," said Mama.   7

Reprinted from TCM 019 Early Childhood Units for Holidays, *Teacher Created Materials, 1992*

Making Little Books *(cont.)*

Out came the Christmas card.
Out came the candy cane.
Out came the Christmas present.
Out came the Christmas tree.
Out came the reindeer.
Out came the elf.

8

"Ho, ho, ho!" said Santa,
and it was Christmas!

9

Reprinted from TCM 019 Early Childhood Units for Holidays, *Teacher Created Materials, 1992*

Mini-books like the Christmas example are effective ways to build students' sight word vocabularies and lead them into reading. Reciting the stories over and over, students practice the art of reading, reinforce sight word recognition skills, and begin to view themselves as readers. Many teachers have students make "book boxes" in the beginning of the school year. Decorating book boxes, made from donated shoe boxes, is not only fun for students but provides them with a place to store their personal, school-made mini-books at home. By the end of the year, students have an assortment of stories they can read and enjoy. This solves many problems at home, as well, as parents have readily-available books that are the appropriate level for their children to read.

As mentioned earlier, games are an appropriate tool to use for practicing sight words. Concentration, bingo, baseball, and word checkers are all enjoyable ways to learn sight words. Students of all ages love playing games. Concentration is played by simply using a set of sight word cards. Two cards for each word must be included in the set. Students can work in pairs or small groups. The cards are placed face-down and students take turns turning two cards over at a time, looking for a match. Students who make a match take another turn until a match is not made. Students quickly learn that this a memory game and employ strategies for remembering the location of each card, as well as the word written on it.

Concentration, bingo, baseball, and word checkers are all enjoyable ways to learn sight words.

For those who are not familiar with word checkers, the game is very similar to the traditional checkers game. Cover the black squares on a checkerboard with sight words. Play the game the same as regular checkers except have students say the word that is placed on the square before a checker is moved to that space.

When selecting words to use in the game format for beginning readers, Manzo and Manzo (1995) indicate one key point to remember. Avoid words that look alike, as what/when, and their/then. Just as with initial teaching of the alphabet, it is best to select words that have clear differences. Words can also be chosen from a theme of study. For example, a bingo game may be made for each season of the year. The game can be played with the whole-class or in small-groups.

Concluding Remarks

It seems obvious that a powerful sight vocabulary is an important resource for readers. Students should be able to recognize words effortlessly so that they may focus on making meaning. Making mini-books and playing games at school can assist students in learning the basic words that comprise much of our language.

Students can also practice sight words as part of their homework.

It is important to note that it is often those words that students do not recognize by sight that contribute most significantly to the meaning of the text. We are talking about content specific words, such as *diphthong*, *schwa*, and *phonemic awareness*, and *penicillin*, *infection*, and *antibiotic*. To deal comfortably with these words, students must use all of the decoding skills presented so far, as well as context clues. Context clues will be the topic of the next chapter.

Context Clues

The English Language

Bryson (1990) tells us,

"But perhaps the single notable characteristic of English—for better and worse—is its deceptive complexity. Nothing in English is quite what it seems. Take the simple word *what*. We use it every day—indeed, every few sentences. But imagine trying to explain to a foreigner what *what* means. It takes the *Oxford English Dictionary* five pages and almost 15,000 words to manage the task. As native speakers, we seldom stop to think just how complicated and illogical English is" (p. 19).

As speakers of English, how did we get so comfortable with an often illogical language? How have we learned to deal with words as mysterious as *what* ? We have met *what* time after time in context. Through repeated exposures to *what* in rich and meaningful settings, which includes listening to predictable books full of predictable language, we know what *what* is about. There is little doubt that *what* cannot be sounded out. The vowel sound just does not work very well. However, when *what* is encountered repeatedly in familiar and enjoyable books, we begin to make *what* our own.

As speakers of English, how did we get so comfortable with an often illogical language?

What is Context?

Context is the tool that ties the decoding process together. Producing students who ask themselves the question, "Does this make sense?" when reading may be the single most important thing teachers do. Context is the tool that allows students to answer this question. This chapter will define context, give further justification for teaching it, supply strategies for teaching it, and present a list of predictable books for enhancing students' understanding and use of it.

When students use context clues, they are using the print surrounding an unfamiliar word to give it meaning and to help pronounce it. Adams (1990) discusses context as follows: "Readers work with context to select (and, when necessary, re-select) the most appropriate meaning of the phrase as a whole" (p. 413). Our statement, and that by Adams, lends credence to the concept that context is the tool which allows students to answer the most important question about what they are reading: "Does this make sense?" Context guides students to not over-rely on phonics and structural analysis. It keeps students from producing sentences such as, "I saw Sue riding a house through the meadow." However, as essential as context is, it cannot stand alone. It must be used in balance with other decoding tools. Students who use context, phonics, structural analysis, and a powerful sight vocabulary as they approach unfamiliar words greatly increase their ability to decode these words and make them their own. Let us look at how context works with other decoding skills to guide students to unlock words. A word to question is *father*. If students used phonics alone, they might produce /fa ther/ with a short /a/, or /fay ther/ with a long /a/ sound. If they used just structural analysis, they might see a compound word and produce /fat her/. But it is when they read a sentence like, "I have hair the same color as my father's," and see *father* in context, that the word and sentence make sense.

> **When students have a firm understanding of the book they are reading, they have created a context and know every word they encounter should fit within the context.**

It must be stressed that the use of context moves well beyond the sentence level. When students have a firm understanding of the book they are reading, they have created a context and know every word they encounter should fit within the context. Students are logical and understand that scary stories have scary words and descriptive tales have descriptive words. It is students who cannot create context that produce sentences such as, "I saw Sue riding a house in the meadow."

All students do not naturally use context. This can be especially true of students who rely too much on sight words or phonics as they decode and who do not have personally valuable reasons for reading. Fortunately, students can be taught to use context. We suggest such instruction start even before they begin to read.

Strategies for Teaching Context Clues

This section will present strategies for producing students who use context successfully. Focus will be on three concepts.

- ◆ We need to develop students who have a reason for reading.
- ◆ We need to produce students who monitor their reading and continually ask themselves the question, "Does this make sense?"
- ◆ We need all of this to begin before students have had formal reading instruction.

Developing Students Who Have a Reason to Read

Students need to view reading as a personally valuable experience. When a student picks up *Miss Nelson is Missing* (Allard, 1977) and says, "I want to read this," the chances are significantly increased that he or she will naturally use context. When a student looks at the cover of *Where the Wild Things Are* (Sendak, 1963) and states, "Wow, look at those monsters!" the chances are great that he or she has developed a rich story context. We suggest guiding students to develop reasons for reading by taking two or three minutes before a story is read to look at the cover together, read the title, examine the illustrations, and ask questions about the story. Initially, as teachers, we should model the question-asking process, then guide students to develop their own questions.

Students need to view reading as a personally valuable experience.

Developing Students who Ask Themselves, "Does this make sense?"

We have said it before, and it is the perfect time to say it again. Asking the question, "Does this make sense?" is an extremely important characteristic of an effective reader. It is not something most readers do consciously. However, when something does not make sense, most individuals quickly stop and carefully examine the troublesome word or sentence. When a student reads, "I saw Sue riding a house in the meadow," we have one of the rare reasons for interrupting a student's reading and asking, "Does that sentence make sense?" There are several strategies for developing "sense-making" students. One that we like is called the cloze technique.

Cloze is a technique in which the reader supplies deleted words in a sentence or passage by using syntactic (grammatical) and semantic (meaning bearing) clues. It guides students to focus on meaning cues rather than just graphic cues. It assists students in using context clues when they can verify the appropriateness of a tentatively decoded word.

Cloze Activities

There is a variety of cloze activities. They are as follows:

◆ Activities where highly predictable words are deleted.

"_____ is a process where students associate sounds with written symbols."

◆ Activities where every .nth (eg. number of your choice) word is deleted.

"Phonics is a process _____ students associate sounds with _____ symbols."

◆ Activities where words are deleted but the initial letter or letter combination is supplied.

"Phonics is a process wh_____ students associate sounds with wr_____ symbols."

◆ Activities where words are deleted but students are given a choice of words to select.

"Phonics is a process wh_____ students associate sounds with written symbols."

          who   where   what

◆ Activities where just selected nouns, adjectives, verbs, etc. are deleted.

"Phonics is a process where _____ associate sounds with written symbols."

Cloze is a technique that enhances students' use and understanding of context.

Cloze is a technique that enhances students' use and understanding of context. However, students use of context develops most easily when they are introduced to the concept early in their literacy development. Toward this goal, children should be read to from the moment they can sit in a parent's lap. The language of literature should run through their heads. The more they hear this language, the more they come to understand how it works. It is the rare student who does not read along with Bill Martin, Jr.'s *Brown Bear, Brown Bear, What Do You See?* (1967) or chime in "even in Australia," when Judith Viorst's *Alexander and the Terrible, Horrible, Not Good, Very Bad Day* (1987), is read.

We have developed a strategy that is particularly effective for developing context in young children. When reading to students,

We have developed a strategy that is particularly effective for developing context in young children. When reading to students, simply make the slightest pause when a highly predictable word is encountered. We have actually seen students lean forward, mouthing the word they know is going to come. When reading *I Know an Old Lady Who Swallowed a Fly* (Rounds, 1990), make a pause just before *die*, in the phrase, "I guess she'll die" and watch what happens. This simple strategy naturally develops a knowledge of context in a child's mind. There is a category of books that best allows this to happen. They are called predictable and pattern books. Some of our favorites follow. Additional sources of predictable and pattern books, as well as instructional strategies, can be found in Rhodes (1981), Cerbus and Rice (1995), and Opitz (1995).

Predictable and Pattern Books

Asch, F.	*Just Like Daddy* (1984, Simon & Schuster)
Carle, E.	*The Very Hungry Caterpillar* (1986, Putnam)
Cook, B.	*The Little Fish that Got Away* (1993, Scholastic)
Eastman, P.D.	*Are You My Mother?* (1986, Random)
Hill, E.	*Where's Spot?* (1994, Puffin)
Hoberman, M.A.	*A House is a House for Me* (1993, Puffin)
Hutchins, P.	*One Hunter* (1986, Morrow)
Kraus, R.	*Herman the Helper* (1987, Simon & Schuster)
Mack, S.	*Ten Bears in My Bed* (1974, Pantheon)
Martin, B.	*Brown Bear, Brown Bear* (1967, Holt)
Martin, B.	*Fire, Fire, Said Mrs. McGuire* (1995, Harcourt)
Numeroff, L.J.	*If You Give a Mouse a Cookie* (1985, Scholastic)
Sendak, M.	*Chicken Soup With Rice* (1986, Scholastic)
Viorst, J.	*Alexander and the Terrible, Horrible, No Good, Very Bad Day* (1987, Macmillan)
West, C.	*Have You Seen the Crocodile?* (1986, HarperCollins)
Wood, A.	*The Napping House* (1991, Harcourt)

Context is the powerful bridge between decoding and comprehension.

Concluding Remarks

Context is the powerful bridge between decoding and comprehension. It is the final piece in the decoding puzzle. It is the central component of students' personal logic of the code, and it guides them to ask the question, "Does what I'm reading make sense?"

This book began by stating our bias about the environment in which students best gain their own logic of the code. It is a balanced environment where students are given authentic reasons to read and write and are systematically provided with instruction that allows them to do so. This type of environment creates momentum in the classroom. Momentum is created when students see a reason for learning what is being taught. They see a reason for coming to school each day. Chall (1967) tells us one of the best ways to stop momentum in a classroom is to focus on having students do unmonitored seatwork, especially with workbooks and drill-type worksheets. *Becoming A Nation of Readers* (1985) tells us it is not unusual to have students doing 1000 worksheets a year. Adams (1990) reports on a longitudinal study of children in a Texas school. In this study, it was found that forty percent of the lower-income fourth graders claimed that they would rather clean their rooms than read. One child stated, "I'd rather clean the mold around the bathtub than read" (p. 5). Dorothy Strickland and Bernice Cullinan in Adams (1990) state,

"If learning is to occur, we must give children good stories that intrigue and engage them; we must give them poetry that sings with the beauty of language; we must enchant them with language play; and we must give them opportunities to write. In short, we must surround them with literature that helps them understand their world and their ability to create meaning" (p. 428).

Give students a reason to read through great books, and then teach them all the necessary decoding skills they need to read these books. To conclude this text, we turn to a simple formula for the complex and important process of producing students who can and do read:

Good literature + good teaching = good readers.

References

Adams, M. J. (1990). <u>Beginning to read: Thinking and learning about print</u>. Cambridge, MA: MIT Press.

Allard, H. (1977). <u>Miss Nelson is Missing</u>. Boston: Houghton Mifflin.

Anderson, R. C., Hiebert, E. H., Scott, J. A., & Wilkerson, J. A. G. (1985). <u>Becoming a nation of readers: The report of the Commission on Reading</u>. Washington DC: The National Institute of Education.

Bailey, M. H. (1967). The utility of phonic generalizations in grades one through six. <u>The Reading Teacher, 20</u>(5), 413–418.

Balmuth, M. (1982). <u>The roots of phonics</u>. New York: Teachers College Press.

Bishop, A. L. (1978). My daughter learns to read. <u>The Reading Teacher, 32</u>(1), 4–6.

Bryson, B. (1990). <u>The mother tongue: English and how it got that way</u>. New York: William Morrow and Company.

Burmeister, L. E. (1968). Usefulness of phonic generalizations. <u>The Reading Teacher, 21</u>(4), 349–356, 360.

Burns, P. C., Roe, B. D., & Ross, E. P. (1996). <u>Teaching reading in today's elementary schools</u>. Boston: Houghton Mifflin.

Carroll, J. B., Davies, P., & Richman, B. (1971). <u>Word frequency book</u>. Boston: Houghton Mifflin.

Cerbus, D. P., & Rice, C. F. (1995). <u>Whole language units for predictable books</u>. Westminster, CA: Teacher Created Materials.

Chall, J. S. (1967). <u>Learning to read: The great debate</u>. New York: McGraw-Hill.

Chaney, J. H. (1993). Alphabet books: Resources for learning. <u>The Reading Teacher, 47</u>(2), 96–104.

Clymer, T. (1963). The utility of phonic generalizations in the primary grades. <u>The Reading Teacher, 16</u>(4), 252–258.

Cunningham, P. M., Moore, S. A., Cunningham, J. W., & Moore, D. W. (1989). <u>Reading in the elementary classroom: Strategies and observations</u>. New York: Longman.

Eeds, M. (1985). Bookwords: Using a beginning word list of high frequency words from children's literature K-3. <u>The Reading Teacher, 38</u>(4), 418–423.

Evans, R. (1967). The usefulness of phonic generalizations above the primary grades. <u>The Reading Teacher, 20</u>(6), 419–425.

Flesch, R. (1955). <u>Why Johnny can't read</u>. New York: Harper and Row.

Fry, E. (1980). The new instant word list. <u>The Reading Teacher, 34</u>(3), 284–289.

Galdone, P. (1973). <u>The little red hen.</u> New York: Scholastic.

Gaskins, R. W., Gaskins, J. C., & Gaskins, I. W. (1991). A decoding program for poor readers - And the rest of the class, too! <u>Language Arts, 68</u>(3), 213–225.

Goodman, K. S. (1972). Reading: A psycholinguistic guessing game. In L. A. Harris, & C. B. Smith (Eds.), <u>Individualized reading instruction: A reader</u>. New York: Holt, Rinehart, & Winston.

Groff, P. (1986). The maturing of phonics instruction. <u>The Reading Teacher, 39</u>(9), 919–923.

Gunning, J. G. (1995). Word building: A strategic approach to the teaching of phonics. <u>The Reading Teacher, 48</u>(6) 484–488.

Huey, E. B. (1908). <u>The psychology and pedagogy of reading</u>. New York: Macmillan.

Manzo, A. V., & Manzo, V. C. (1995). <u>Teaching children to be literate: A reflective approach.</u> Fort Worth, TX: Harcourt Brace College Publishers.

Martin, B., Jr., & Archambault, J. (1989). <u>Chicka chicka boom boom</u>. New York: Simon & Schuster.

Martin, B., Jr. (1967). <u>Brown bear, brown bear, what do you see</u>? New York: Henry Holt.

Opitz, M. F. (1995). <u>Getting the most from predictable books</u>. New York: Scholastic.

Rhodes, L. K. (1981). I can read! Predictable books as a resource for reading and writing instruction. <u>The Reading Teacher, 34</u>(5), 511–518.

Rounds, G. (1990). <u>I know an old lady who swallowed a fly</u>. New York: Holiday.

Ryan, C. D. (1995). <u>Teaching basic skills through literature</u>. Westminster, CA: Teacher Created Materials.

Sendak, M. (1963). <u>Where the wild things are</u>. New York: Scholastic.

Smith, N. B. (1967). <u>American Reading Instruction</u>. Newark, NJ: International Reading Association.

Stahl, S. A. (1992). Saying the 'p' word: Nine guidelines for exemplary phonics instruction. <u>The Reading Teacher, 45</u>(8), 618–625.

Stanovich, K. E. (1986). Matthew effects in reading: Some consequences of individual differences in the acquisition of literacy. <u>Reading Research Quarterly, 21</u>(3) 360–406.

Viorst, J. (1987). <u>Alexander and the terrible, horrible, no good, very bad day.</u> New York: Macmillan.

Wylie, R. E., & Durrell, D. D. (1970). Teaching vowels through phonograms. <u>Elementary English, 47</u>(6), 787–791.

Yopp, H. K. (1988). The validity and reliability of phonemic awareness tests. <u>Reading Research Quarterly, 23</u>(2), 159–177.

Yopp, H. K. (1992). Developing phonemic awareness in young children. <u>The Reading Teacher, 45</u>(9), 696–704.

Yopp, H. K. (1995a). Read-aloud books for developing phonemic awareness: An annotated bibliography. <u>The Reading Teacher, 49</u>(6), 538–543.

Yopp, H. K. (1995b). A test for assessing phonemic awareness in young children. <u>The Reading Teacher, 49</u>(1), 20–29.

Teacher Created Materials
Resource List

TCM 147 Activities for Any Literature Unit

TCM 019 Early Childhood Units for Holidays
TCM 202 Early Childhood Units for the Alphabet
TCM 204 Early Childhood Units for Favorite Tales
TCM 206 Early Childhood Units for Predictable Books

TCM 353 Literature Activities for Reluctant Readers—Primary
TCM 354 Literature Activities for Reluctant Readers—Intermediate

TCM 436 Strega Nona Literature Unit
TCM 525 Where the Wild Things Are Literature Unit
TCM 536 Johnny Appleseed Literature Unit
TCM 538 Madeline Literature Unit
TCM 540 The Cat in the Hat Literature Unit
TCM 543 The Polar Express Literature Unit

TCM 773 Language Arts Assessment Grades 1–2
TCM 777 Language Arts Assessment Grades 3–4
TCM 781 Language Arts Assessment Grades 5–6

TCM 791 Teaching Basic Skills Through Literature: Phonics
TCM 792 Teaching Basic Skills Through Literature: Language Arts

TCM 862 November Monthly Activities—Early Childhood

Teacher Created Materials
Resource List *(cont.)*

Easy Phonics Readers
TCM 2010 Skate, Kate, Skate
TCM 2011 The Green Seed
TCM 2012 Mice on Ice
TCM 2013 My Old Gold Boat
TCM 2014 Duke the Blue Mule
TCM 2015 Gail's Paint Pail
TCM 2016 My Cap
TCM 2017 Brett My Pet
TCM 2018 Will Bill?
TCM 2019 Dot's Pot
TCM 2020 My Truck and My Pup
TCM 2021 This is Fred

Professional Organizations

International Reading Association
800 Barksdale Road
P. O. Box 8139
Newark, DE 19714-8139
1-800-336-READ

National Council of Teachers of English
1111 Kenyon Road
Urbana, IL 61801
1-800-369-6283